MORE BOOKS FROM THE SAGER GROUP & NEOTEXT

The Stacks Reader Series

The Cheerleaders: A True Story by E. Jean Carroll

An American Family: A True Story by Daniel Voll

Flesh and Blood: A True Story by Peter Richmond

An Accidental Martyr: A True Story by Chip Brown

Death of a Playmate: A True Story by Teresa Carpenter

The Detective: And Other True Stories by Walt Harrington

General Interest

The Stories We Tell: Classic True Tales by America's Greatest Women Journalists

New Stories We Tell: True Tales by America's New Generation of Great Women Journalists

Newswomen: Twenty-Five Years of Front-Page Journalism

The Devil & John Holmes: And Other True Stories of Drugs, Porn and Murder by Mike Sager

The Orphan's Daughter, A Novel by Jan Cherubin

Lifeboat No. 8: Surviving the Titanic by Elizabeth Kaye

Hunting Marlon Brando: A True Story by Mike Sager

The Swamp: Deceit and Corruption in the CIA (An Elizabeth Petrov Thriller) (Book 1) by Jeff Grant

A Boy and His Dog in Hell: And Other True Stories by Mike Sager

See our entire library at TheSagerGroup.net

The Deadliest Man Alive: Count Dante, The Mob, and the War for American Martial Arts

Copyright © 2022 Benji Feldheim

All rights reserved. No part of this publication may be reproduced, stored in a retrieval system, or transmitted, in any form or by any means, electronic, mechanical, photocopying, recording, or otherwise, without the prior written permission of the publisher. Published in the United States of America.

Cover design and cover art by WBYK.com.au
Interior design by Siori Kitajima, PatternBased.com

Cataloging-in-Publication data for this book is available from the Library of Congress.
ISBN-13:
eBook: 978-1-950154-74-6
Paperback: 978-1-950154-75-3

Published by The Sager Group LLC
(TheSagerGroup.net)
In cooperation with NeoText
(NeoTextCorp.com)

THE DEADLIEST MAN ALIVE

Count Dante, The Mob, and the War for American Martial Arts

BENJI FELDHEIM

Before he became Count Dante, The Deadliest Man Alive, master of Dim Mak, The Death Touch...

Before he helped form the event that became widely known as the United States Karate Association Grand National Championship...

Before he became Supreme Grand Master of the Black Dragon Fighting Society...

Before he started his own dojo and dared to train Black folks and women...

Before he incited the deadly dojo war in Chicago...

Before he opened a hair salon and coiffed the hair of Playboy Bunnies...

Before he owned a string of occult and porno bookstores...

Before he bought a pet lion and walked it around the streets on a leash like a dog...

Before he took to wearing a cape and carrying a walking stick embossed with gold leaf...

Before he started selling his patented fighting system—capable of killing a man with a single blow—in comic books...

Before he was—or wasn't?—involved with the Mob...

Before he did—or did not—help to organize Chicago's record-setting Purolator Heist from which $1.5 million was never recovered...

Before he got hooked on cocaine, became even more bizarre, and died mysteriously...

He was John Keehan.

CONTENTS

Preface 1
Early Days 5
My Hand Is my Sword: Robert Trias 11
Breaking the Color Barrier 13
The 1963 World Karate Tournament 17
The Count Begins to Emerge 21
The Lion 23
1964 World Karate Tournament 25
The Fallout with Trias 29
Karate Doesn't Work in a Phone Booth or a Prison Cell:
Arthur Rapkin's Story 31
Blasting Caps 37
Rapkin vs. The Bull 41
Count Dante and The World's Deadliest Fighting Secrets 45
Enter the Dragon Lady 51
The Dojo War 57
Meeting Bob Cooley 63
"I can catch a bullet in my bare hand." 67
The Chicago Outfit 71
Rapkin and The White 75
Fall River 77
The Purolator Heist 79
The Taunton Death Matches 85
Purolator Fallout and Dante's Death 89
Juan R. Dante Keehan 93
Epilogue 95
Where They Are Now 99

Acknowledgements 101
About the Author 103
About the Publishers 104

PREFACE

At six feet one inch, with a strong and domineering posture that made him appear larger than he was, John Keehan radiated charisma and menace, the archetypical alpha male. His blue eyes were intensely focused, some used the word "piercing" to describe the way he seemed to be looking not so much at you as through you, appraisingly and then into the distance beyond, as if he was always calculating new ways to win fights, new moves to make, new places to go, new ways to make money, and new ways to dominate his environment the way he could dominate on the mats, or in an alley. To live his life differently than all the run-of-the-mill humans he'd see every day on the street, sleepwalking through their lives like zombies, like losers—weaklings full of nothing but lame excuses and hollow dreams—what the fuck, had they even tried?

From his first time in a dojo, it was clear that Keehan had a talent for martial arts and a taste for domination. Skilled in boxing, karate, and other Asian disciplines, he quickly rose through the ranks of established martial arts schools and opened his own dojo by age twenty-four.

In time, however, the rising star would be ostracized by the martial arts establishment of his times, much of it built by World War II veterans who picked up fighting styles while overseas during the war, and Japanese Americans who'd survived internment camps. At the time, these masters preferred teaching strictly regimented and rehearsed forms and katas, concentrating on techniques, not fighting. Often, only white and Asian men were allowed in the classes.

But Keehan was controversy in action. He opened his dojo to Blacks and women; some would start their own martial arts school, creating a lineage for people who otherwise wouldn't have had the chance to learn karate.

And besides teaching technique, Keehan concentrated on training his students for street fights. "You can't do a roundhouse kick in a phone booth," he liked to say.

Keehan taught his students how to get in close, claw at the eyeballs, attack the groin. His classes combined technique drilling with hard sparring. Often, he would recreate real-life self-defense scenarios, using weapons, or pitting six students against one, just to make the training as realistic as possible. At tournaments, his students were more brutal than those from the formalist schools and often won, leaving many calling foul—and further deepening the divide between himself and more traditional martial arts establishments.

When not pursuing his interests in martial arts, Keehan dabbled in a curious assortment of other career pursuits. He worked as a hairdresser, skilled enough to be hired by Playboy Enterprises to coif the hair of its Chicago Bunnies. He worked as the director of a wig and hairpiece firm, and as a beauty consultant. Eventually, he would also own adult bookstores and other stores selling occult paraphernalia. His used car lot on Chicago's South Side was one of two enterprises that hinted at a connection between himself and the Chicago-based Mafia. The other would prove to be the greatest heist in Chicago history.

No matter what role he was playing, Dante carried himself with the arrogance of a man who knew his very presence was a lethal force. You could tell right away that he didn't need much provocation. Though adored by the dozens or even hundreds of loyal students he had schooled, Dante was disliked by at least as many who liked him.

As the years went by, Keehan would take his act to the next level, morphing himself into the outlandish, comic book persona the world would come to know through his ads in comic books: The World's Deadliest Fighting Secrets Can Be Yours! (*Act now and your authentic Black Dragon Fighting Society membership card will be rushed to you at no extra cost!*)

As Count Dante, the ginger Keehan dyed his hair jet black. He often wore a cape with a collar flipped up like Dracula. Under the cape, in super-hero style, leotards revealed his muscular form; a 24-carat gold-leaf embossed cane completed the outfit. To sculpt his trademark beard, with its sinister swoops and carved points—so elaborate it looked as if it had been carefully drawn onto his face with a magic marker—Keehan used hair removal powder, which left the exposed skin on his cheeks raw and pink. He drove a Cadillac Eldorado with his personal crest emblazoned on the doors, two growling lions. For a while, he kept a lion as a pet and would be seen walking it along the streets of Chicago, using a length of grade 100 high-strength steel straight chain as a leash.

As both Keehan and Dante, he was never without a woman by his side. Like the comic book hero he was shaping himself to be, he fancied that women wanted him and men wanted to be like him.

And the more people bought into his projection, the more he needed to prove.

To some, Keehan/Dante is remembered as a martial arts pioneer and a fighter against prejudice; he was among the first karate instructors to allow people of color and women to become black belts in his dojo. With his free combination of styles and unleashed aggression, he helped sow the seeds for the type of modern mixed martial arts that is so prevalent today. A few years after his death, martial arts tournaments in all styles upped the ante, allowing protective gear and a higher level of contact. Further into the 1980s, fighters from different styles would face each other in the first versions of what we know today as the Ultimate Fighting Championship's Octagon.

But to others he was a selfish opportunist who took advantage of those around him, a peacocking, big-talking scam artist who always remained one step ahead of the law. As he completed his transformation into Count Dante, his behavior became increasingly outlandish and dangerous. Throughout his life, the people closest to Dante would reach their limit with his antics and would distance themselves from him out of fear.

As wrote D. David Dreis, who served as managing editor of *Black Belt* magazine in 1969: "He was not a villain as many people supposed . . . but he does villainous things."

One thing was sure. When Count Dante walked in a room, you believed anything was possible.

EARLY DAYS

John Timothy Keehan was born on February 4, 1939, to Jack and Dorothy Keehan. His father was an OB/GYN and served as president of the Ashland State Bank. The bank was described by Bloomberg as "a full-service bank that accepted deposits, made loans, and provided other services for the public," until it merged with the Austin State Bank in the 1980s. Keehan grew up in the Beverly neighborhood of Chicago's South Side, his family in an "upper-income bracket," he told writer Massad Ayoob in an interview for *Black Belt*.

Almost exactly a year after John Keehan entered the world, Tommy Gregory was born. He grew up near Ninety-Second and Loomis streets in the Brainerd neighborhood, just a few blocks away from the Keehans' home. In 1947, around the time Gregory was in second grade, he was walking near a prairie patch close to their homes and saw two kids beating up on Keehan.

"I ran over there as they were just pounding him on the ground. But I joined him and we turned the tables. We beat the shit out of those guys and John and I became friends."

The Gregory family didn't have much money; the Keehans were well off. Dorothy Keehan would often give the boys money to fund their escapades around downtown. They'd hop on the L train, smoke cigars, hit the arcades, and get themselves into minor mischief, Gregory said.

"With a dollar or two back then, we could do anything we wanted. We'd spend all day running around downtown."

On Friday nights, Dorothy would take Tommy and John out to dinner in fancy restaurants, using the opportunities to school them in proper manners.

When Gregory was fourteen, he and his sister Joan, who was friends with John's sister, Diane, joined the Keehans on a summer trip to a private island in Canada for two weeks. Some nights, Gregory would stay at the Keehans' three-flat on Bishop Street for the night. The basement was their rumpus room. They'd goof off, watch TV, play war games with rubber pellet guns. "We were lucky we never shot each other's eyes out," Gregory said. There was also an old set of weights. Almost every time, they would lift.

"It was always important to John to be strong," Gregory said. "I don't think he ever forgot that beating when I met him. He never wanted it to happen again."

Jack Keehan was just as generous and kind to Gregory, the kind of doctor who would give free care to his more needy patients. The only time Gregory remembers Jack getting mad at the boys was years ago when they shot out a neighbor's window with a BB gun. "He just took the gun from us and bent it in two," Gregory said. "I never saw him raise a hand against John. And that time with the BB gun, it was an accident."

Even if Jack was deeply relaxed in his recliner after a long day, when Gregory arrived looking hungry, as he sometimes did, Jack would haul himself out and grab the young man something from the kitchen. Then Jack and John and Gregory would sit around the table, enjoying a snack and shooting the shit like the old friends they were.

The Keehans' affection for Gregory would last a lifetime. Years later, when he was twenty-three, Gregory was visiting Keehan at home. The two were still close. Gregory showed Dorothy a string of pearls he'd just bought for a girl he was in love with.

"You can't afford those," Dorothy Keehan told him. Then she left the room and returned with a stack of cash to cover the pearls. Without saying another word, she placed the bills in his hand.

Gregory remembers Keehan as a strong student in school. He'd recall everything he read in any book, even after one read. He could learn and apply skills just by reading guides to them, as if the information in the words jumped from the pages right into his brain and body.

"He was just so damn smart," Gregory said. "He could do anything. He was always calculating angles, seeing if there was a way he could come out even higher on top. With him, there was always an easier and better way than what other people were doing."

Keehan was drawn to the mysterious as early as age twelve. Gregory remembers him reading about ways people could fake their death for long enough to convince others that they were gone, only to walk away afterward and live a new life under a new identity. "It was all about controlling your breath to the point where you could appear lifeless," Gregory said.

For a time, Gregory recalled, Keehan wanted to be an opera singer and took opera lessons at a conservatory. "He had a powerful voice. I guess it was like everything else about him: he just wanted everything louder, faster, stronger, more intense. With John there was only one gear—full out."

But what drew him most was fighting. He started training at thirteen at Johnny Coulon's boxing gym on East Sixty-Third Street and Woodlawn Avenue. While at Mount Carmel High School, on 6410 South Dante Avenue, Keehan took up wrestling.

Early one morning in 1957, when Keehan was eighteen, he and Gregory found themselves joyriding with three other guys in Jack Keehan's 1957 Oldsmobile convertible, doing more than 100 miles per hour on a street near where they lived.

"We were racing all over the place. He was going so goddamned fast. He ran it right into a prairie plot just like the one near his house where I first met him, but with rocks and cement all over the place. We flew up into the air, crashed, came to a dead stop. We probably bent the roof with our heads. We couldn't open the doors. We had to break the windows to get out. Everybody was bleeding. We just limped back home. He never said anything about it. I never knew if his parents ever found out."

"In those days in Chicago, it was pretty hard to stay out of trouble," Keehan told the writer Ayoob. "Everyone was always getting into fights. I was always very interested in body building, weightlifting, boxing, wrestling, judo—anything having to do with fighting and training."

When the pair were old enough to pass for twenty-one, they liked to dress up nice and hit the bars and jazz clubs in nearby Black neighborhoods—nobody there was checking ID. They were often the only white people at the clubs. They didn't mind. It seemed to be the point. They would mingle and dance with the women who were willing. One night at a club on State Street near Seventy-Ninth, they stumbled upon Fats Domino at the piano. Hardly anyone was there that night, Gregory said. "We were just mesmerized. It was one of the few times I ever saw John just mesmerized by something."

Sometimes the guys would take their dates to Jackson Park, just south of the Museum of Science and Industry along Lake Michigan. They would "borrow" a dinghy that wasn't locked down and row out to Keehan's father's boat, which was moored offshore. On one outing, their dates got into a fight and started swinging oars at one another, capsizing the boat and sending all four of them into the lake.

Gregory also remembers Keehan being a clothes horse who didn't mind spending his parents' money.

"He wouldn't just have one sweater, he had ten freaking sweaters," Gregory said. "If you bought a pair of black pants and he'd like them, he'd have every goddamn color there was. He would buy everything."

Gregory remembers Keehan using his father's credit to bankroll his spending. When one of the cars he drove broke down around Sixty-Third Street and Ashland Avenue, he just pulled over to the side, got out, opened the trunk, took his stuff out and walked away.

"He just left that car right on the side of the road," Gregory said.

Keehan joined the Marine Corps Reserve after high school. The only released military records on his enlisted time show that he reported for training on June 3, 1958, and was honorably discharged one year later. Keehan said he later enlisted in the army. He told Ayoob he "killed at least twenty-five people" while serving in the armed forces.

He also told others he had been a guerrilla fighter under Raul Castro in Cuba's Sierra Maestra mountains.

"There is always a surge in not being killed yourself, in being a survivor," he told Ayoob. "But I do not get any type of sexual, spiritual, physical, or psychological thrill out of killing somebody. I believe in the human spirit and the individual soul."

Keehan told *Black Belt* he learned aikido from a person named "Commander Cramer," and that he studied judo and jiu jitsu in Chicago at Gene Wyka's Chicago Karate and Judo Center. While serving in the military, he said he spent "almost all of my time out of boot camp, in the Far East" picking up different fighting skills.

"I studied hapkido, tang soo do, moo duk kwan, tae kwon do, Thai boxing, Chinese boxing. When I was over there, they didn't know what Kung Fu was. They called it Chinese boxing. . . . I never stayed with one school, see, because I felt it hindered me."

Keehan told *Black Belt* he studied under as many as twenty different martial arts instructors. "I don't think any were any good. But you know, my greatest instructor was myself. You learn more because if you have an instructor, he is doing your thinking and you've got to think for yourself. The greatest instructor I ever had was actual application in the street and looking in a mirror."

In a file on Keehan released by the FBI in response to a Freedom of Information Act request, records show he was dishonorably discharged from the army for possession of marijuana and absence without official leave for the whole month of February in 1960. According to a military disciplinary record, Keenan was imprisoned for an unspecified amount of time before being released. "The prisoner is an unreliable informant, and many discrepancies and inconsistencies were noted in the history." The disciplinary record also listed that Keehan had crashed cars, destroyed property, shot at a friend's car with a pistol, and hit himself in the head with a pistol.

Gregory said Keehan's discharge resulted from his growing disenchantment with the army, and he was "doing every delinquent thing he could think of to get out."

The FBI file also noted that on April 1, 1957, prior to his enlistment in the Marine Corps, Keehan was arrested by Chicago police and charged with "selling a firearm." The charge was dismissed in court five days later.

On March 19, 1960, the file said, Keehan was arrested by the Chicago police on a charge of "investigation-narcotics." Two days later, the charge against Keehan was dropped.

In response to a Freedom of Information Act request, the Chicago Police Department said they have no existing records of any contact with Keehan.

Late in 1960, Keehan enrolled in the University of Miami but never earned a degree. Gregory remembers him talking about trips to Cuba.

Gregory, who also enlisted in the marines around the same time as Keehan, was himself honorably discharged. Thereafter, Gregory started working in Phoenix as a construction contractor.

One day in August 1961, the two old friends were talking on the phone about Gregory's new town.

"Is there a karate school over there in Phoenix?" Keehan asked.

"Yeah, I think there's one nearby."

"Okay, I'm coming."

He arrived a few days later.

MY HAND IS MY SWORD: ROBERT TRIAS

It turned out the school belonged to none other than Robert A. Trias, considered one of America's foremost karate pioneers. Trias was credited with opening America's very first karate school in 1946.

Trias was stationed on the island of Tulagi in the Solomon Islands during World War II while serving in the US Navy, according to an April 1976 profile of Trias in *Black Belt* magazine by Sergio Ortiz. He was training for the navy's middleweight boxing title when he noticed a Chinese missionary named Tung Gee Hsing would watch him exercise. Trias said the small man was a fan of American boxing and that he was imitating Trias's moves on his own. Hsing kept "pestering" Trias to train with him until Trias finally relented, he told *Black Belt*.

"I called all my friends to see me kill this little man," Trias told *Black Belt*. "And I asked him if he wanted to spar with gloves and he said it really didn't matter. Well, before you know it, he was giving me the biggest thrashing of my life. He kept pointing out how he could easily kill me if he wanted and, right there and then, I asked him to teach me."

Trias brought his new fighting skills back home. In late 1945, shortly before Trias left the navy, he began teaching martial arts in his backyard. In 1946, he opened his first dojo in Phoenix. It became the first public karate school operated by a Caucasian on the US mainland. In 1956 he wrote *The Hand is my Sword: A Karate Handbook*, considered the first book about karate published in the United States.

Trias also served as an officer of the Arizona Highway Patrol Division from 1946 to 1961, where he used his self-defense knowledge on duty and taught useful techniques to his fellow officers, some of whom began training in his dojo. In 1948 he founded the United States Karate Association (USKA), the first karate organization on the American mainland.

Recognizing a prodigy when he saw one, Trias ended up training Keehan personally. The strong and athletic Keehan received his green belt one month later, in September 1961. The men would have an ongoing relationship for the next few years. Trias wanted to get the USKA set up in the Midwest, and he found a student who could help him do just that.

"I used to like John quite a bit," Trias told Ayoob in a *Black Belt* interview. "When he was with us, he was very conscientious—a good student. He applied himself well. He used to motor to Phoenix every year to study at my school, spending three or four months at a time."

Keehan would teach karate during the summer months in Chicago at Gene Wyka's Judo and Karate Center, then winter in Phoenix and train at Trias's dojo. Within two years, Keehan would earn a black belt from Trias and would help him start expanding the USKA.

By 1962, Keehan had opened his own dojo, the Imperial Academy of Fighting Arts at 1020 North Rush Street, right above Mister Kelly's night club. The stage at Mister Kelly's was known for breaking race barriers at the time. Bette Midler, Barbra Streisand, and Woody Allen performed in the same space as Richard Pryor, Ella Fitzgerald, and Herbie Hancock. It was a nightlife lightning rod for Chicago in the 1960s and 1970s. Just above Mister Kelly's, Keehan was also breaking norms in his karate classes, both in integration and in technique.

Keehan tapped Gregory for his construction skills. Together the two men added fluorescent lights and wall mirrors and painted the interior. Two bathrooms were installed, for men and women. For a more professional appearance, a front desk was built at the entrance. At night, Gregory slept on a rollaway bed at the dojo. While Keehan taught classes himself in the beginning, in time he wasn't around as much and his more advanced students, like Doug Dwyer and Jim Koncevic, would teach, Gregory said.

Keehan was on his way, building a name for himself and a following.

BREAKING THE COLOR BARRIER

As the 1960s continued, Keehan and Gregory continued their practice of hanging out on the African American side of the segregated city. The epicenter of their nightlife was Sixty-Third Street, described by documentarian Floyd Webb, who is creating a film about Keehan called *The Search for Count Dante*, as "the center of Black Chicago" at the time.

Also nearby was Johnny Coulon's boxing gym, where Keehan had trained as a kid. Exposed to Black people at Coulon's gym and in neighborhoods near where he grew up—particularly Black kids his own age—Keehan would acquire a lifetime appreciation of living in a diverse environment.

Robert C. Brown, a Black man, learned of the unstated color barrier that existed in martial arts when he was first looking to train and was stymied in his attempts. He couldn't find anyone in all of Chicago willing to work with him.

"Keehan didn't care what color I was. He readily accepted me and was glad to have me," Brown said in an interview with Webb prior to Brown's death in 2015.

Brown said he witnessed Keehan arguing with his landlord, who was threatening to kick him out of his dojo space because he was allowing Black people to train. Keehan didn't back down.

Of his fighting skill, Brown said: "John was possibly the most powerful person I've ever met. John could slap you on the shoulder and break your arm. . . . He had this motto: practice it until you can do it. In his mind the secret was relentless work on your craft."

Ray Cooper saw an ad for Keehan's school in a local paper and stopped by. As it happened, he chose to visit on a day when students were engaged in a small, in-school tournament. Keehan asked Cooper if he wanted to compete, and he said yes. Cooper, who had trained for several years with his brother, a military veteran, beat all the white, purple, and brown belts in the classroom. Immediately, Keehan took him on as a student.

"All my memories of John are good memories," Cooper said in an interview with Webb. "He was always very warm and very kind."

Kenny Williams had a background in judo before joining Keehan's school on Rush Street. Looking back almost fifty years, Williams still remembers being impressed with Keehan's ability to break bricks.

"Keehan always taught us to get in close, to focus on that, and not get hung up on how big our opponent was," Williams said. "He always said that you never know what might happen in the streets, and you have to be ready for anything."

Alvin Linzy studied under one of Keehan's students and is head of the United States Tao-Jitsu Federation. He occasionally saw Keehan at the school and around the South Side.

"Keehan was known to be one of the baddest guys in the world. Same with his students," Linzy said. "Martial arts was prejudiced then. There were no Black black belts in this city. Johnny Keehan made the first Black men black belts in Chicago. Trias told him he needed to take them back and Keehan told him no way. That might have been the beginning of a rift between those two.

"I remember Keehan walking down the street like he owned it. He wasn't scared of shit. I always admired Keehan. I'd see him in the martial arts magazines. A lot of people wanted to follow in his footsteps and be like him."

Preston Baker became a student in 1965 of Jimmy Jones Jr., who studied under Keehan. Baker described Keehan as a renegade because he was willing to support and train Black students who went on to start their own schools, like Jones and Robert Brown. Baker went on to start Baker's Dojo of Karate, with his brothers, Otis and Eddie. The school still functions today.

"Jones's classes were tough because that's how Keehan trained him," Baker said. "Keehan would beat you down in an instant. He put a lot of emphasis in his hands, clawing and scratching and all of that. Some of his opponents would come off the floor with their faces bloodied; not the kind of thing you used to see very often in a karate tournament. But with Keehan's method, he wasn't trying to be showy. The emphasis was on showing people how to defend themselves against anything."

THE 1963 WORLD KARATE TOURNAMENT

Dojo master Trias had found not just an apt pupil in Keehan, but also someone who could help enact his vision for the US Karate Association, taking martial arts instruction and larger scale tournaments beyond Arizona and into the Midwest.

In 1963, working together, Keehan and Trias would host the first national karate tournament in the United States, the World Karate Tournament, at the University of Chicago Fieldhouse in Chicago's Hyde Park neighborhood. If Trias was already on the map, this was the event that brought the first widespread attention to Keehan. In 1966, the event would be retitled the US Karate Association Nationals; in 1968 there was another name change, to USKA Grand Nationals.

"Until the late 1960s, competitions were incestuous," said martial arts writer Ayoob. "Tae kwon do fought tae kwon do. The grapplers never met the strikers. That paradigm didn't change until the late '60s, when John came in. John had been a practitioner of *mixed* martial arts. In his techniques you would see everything from Burmese bondo to the Chinese forms to jiu jitsu and aikido. He brought publicity and notoriety to the art, and every kid who saw his ad in a comic book pictured himself in a dojo."

The first USKA tournament was held on July 28, 1963. Many martial arts stars of the time attended, including Ed Parker, Jhoon Rhee, and Bruce Lee. Also among them was Bob Wall, who would appear opposite Lee in *Enter the Dragon* as the bottle-smashing villain O'Hara.

It was clear that the energetic Keehan had done the lion's share of the work and planning for the event. Wall was impressed that even though there was so much prejudice in martial arts back then, Keehan was willing to put excellent Black athletes in the forefront.

The very next Monday after attending the tournament, Jones went to one of Keehan's schools and signed up to start training with Keehan. It was Jones's first exposure to karate. "I was so very impressed with what I'd seen, after watching self-defense and kata form, brick-breaking, all forms of fighting, I decided to visit the school as soon as possible," Jones said in an interview with Floyd Webb.

Jones watched Keehan attempt to break a brick during the tournament with his bare hand. The brick remained intact, leaving Keehan's hand broken. But Keehan tried again with the same hand and succeeded in breaking the brick. Jones told Webb he'd never seen anyone do that before.

"[The] 1963 World's Tournament was the first big tournament where different styles got together," said Brown, in an interview with Floyd Webb. In all, about 250 martial artists competed.

One of the outstanding competitors that year was AlGene Caraulia. Though he was a brown belt, Caraulia had been practicing martial arts for close to a decade leading up to the tournament. He defeated a black belt to become the event's grand champion.

Caraulia studied aikido and jiu jitsu. He also studied a hybrid form of karate called Kajukenbo, which combined judo, jiu jitsu, kenpo, and boxing. Caraulia moved from his birth home in Hawaii to the US mainland in 1959 and continued to immerse himself in martial arts as he made his way from California to Michigan to Chicago in the early 1960s.

Caraulia taught classes at Wyka's Chicago Judo and Karate Center at about the same time as Keehan, though at a different location. Keehan was at the Seventy-Ninth Street and Ashland Avenue location; Caraulia taught at Forty-Second Street and Archer Avenue.

"John and I were never friends; we were colleagues," Caraulia said.

"I don't believe I ever saw him perform any real martial arts, but he was a great talker and motivator. He did have great black belts who studied under him. I think he just always needed people to admire him, so that became his focus, rather than accomplishing for the sake of accomplishing."

Woodrow Edgell first met Keehan right after the first World Karate Tournament in 1963. Edgell, then twenty-four years old, had been practicing karate, aikido, and judo since he was a teen, and he knew of Keehan by reputation. He had read about him in a three-page spread in *Black Belt* in 1963 that described Keehan as one of the country's top karate instructors.

"John was so charismatic that he could almost hypnotize you if you let him," Edgell said.

Edgell, a brown belt in karate, went to the dojo on Rush Street to learn from Keehan, but eventually Keehan started learning skills from Edgell too. Keehan offered to train Edgell privately in karate in exchange for one-on-one instructions from him in aikido and other disciplines. The only rule was that Edgell had to keep those sessions a secret.

"He told me it would look bad if people knew he was learning from a lower belt," Edgell said. "But he understood that you could learn a lot from people around you regardless of status if you just kept an open mind."

Even so, "John was a great person in a lot of ways, but great people make mistakes and he made a few," Edgell said. "Far as I'm concerned, he was one of my closest friends and a person that I will never forget. And to this day, I still have a tremendous amount of respect for John."

At the dojos, Edgell also got to know Jim Koncevic.

"Jim was a fantastic person," Edgell said. "He was extremely talented in martial arts, first earning a black belt in judo and then in karate. He worshipped Keehan."

Edgell trained a few times at Koncevic's school. Edgell said he still remembers how intense Koncevic's routines could be.

"Koncevic was an extremely good fighter and could be a rough one," Edgell said. "But he would try to avoid a fight if possible. Now, he wouldn't back down either, but he didn't go around picking the fights."

Koncevic had a clean-cut look to him, especially when he would wear chunky-style glasses. Edgell would tease him that he looked like Clark Kent with the glasses on, but when he took them off, he could be a stand-in for Superman.

"He seemed happy-go-lucky every time I was around him," Edgell said. "He would try to talk John out of doing something he shouldn't, like if John heard someone from another school was talking bad about him. John would get furious, and Jim would say 'let's just go talk to them.' "

Edgell noticed that Koncevic was capable of following competition rules and rarely argued with judges even if he disagreed with their decisions. Keehan, on the other hand, would argue vehemently if he felt a judge was being unfair, going as far as challenging them to a fight, Edgell said.

Aside from the demonstrations he gave and all the street brawls he managed to get himself involved in, the only sanctioned competitive fight on Keehan's record is a brief match with Gary Alexander at the North American Championships at Madison Square Garden in 1963. Keehan was disqualified for punching Alexander in the groin.

THE COUNT BEGINS TO EMERGE

One day not long after the tournament, Gregory went to see Keehan at one of his apartments. To his surprise, Keehan's place was filled with what he estimated to be $10,000 worth of new clothing.

"He had racks of clothes all over, clothes everywhere," Gregory said.

The contrast wasn't lost on Gregory: while Keehan could show off indulgent wardrobe additions, Gregory was still sleeping on a rollaway bed in the Rush Street dojo.

Gregory stayed involved with Keehan for a time, even starting a home painting business with him. Keehan's whole idea for the painting business was to quote lower prices than other painters. Gregory was skeptical at first, but it worked well enough that they could hire a few other painters to work for them, and they made decent money.

Keehan spent his cash as soon as it was earned. Gregory saved. Within the next two years, Gregory started taking contracting jobs himself, planting the seed to step away from Keehan's world. He bought a few properties to rent out and slowly moved out from under Keehan's shadow.

Meanwhile, Keehan began to hire himself out as a bouncer at bars on the South Side of Chicago.

"John would show up in a beret and a pink shirt some nights," Webb said. "Basically, he did that to set the tone so that somebody would see him in the beret and the pink shirt and start some shit with him. John would make a big show of taking that person out in a matter of seconds, and it was a peaceful evening after that."

Keehan found other ways to leverage the dojo space on Rush Street during the early 1960s. Twice a week, he would sublet space at the dojo on Rush to a fencing group. At other times, it was rented out by the Patricia Stevens Modeling School.

During this time, he met Christa Konrath, a receptionist at the Stevens school. The two later started dating in the early 1970s and remained together all the way up until his death in 1975. It is not known if they legally married, but throughout their association he called her his wife. She is listed as such on Keehan's death certificate.

Always looking for a new way to make a buck, Keehan opened a gift shop and a jewelry store in addition to his beauty parlor, dojo, and other interests. Later into the 1970s, he ran a mail-order business selling hardware and other home items. By some accounts, the mail-order business personnel were all nuns from a local church.

"He didn't trust anybody to handle money for him," Gregory said. "He figured the nuns would be honest. He made a lot of money doing that home business. He was Amazon before Amazon."

THE LION

One day early into 1964 while Gregory was staying with Keehan at his apartment, Keehan walked in cradling under his arm what looked like a very large kitten. Turned out he'd purchased a female lion cub from a zoo in southern Illinois.

"Even that young, it'd tear you up if you didn't keep an eye on her," Gregory said. Early on they would hold all four of the lion's legs and feed her milk with a baby bottle. Keehan named her Aurelia; he told Gregory the name meant "golden one."

Often Gregory would hook a leash to Aurelia's collar and take her on walks. "It'd just walk down the street like I was walking a dog," Gregory said. "People would stop in their tracks. I met a lot of people because of that lion." Gregory fed her frozen horse meat he acquired from a feed house.

One time, at Keehan's request, Gregory drove the lion all the way to Phoenix. For safety, he kept the leash tied to the coat holder over the door. At one point, during a stop for gas, Aurelia stuck her head out the window toward a man pumping gas on the other side of the island. One look, and the man took off running down the street.

On several occasions, the lion defecated in the car while Gregory was driving.

"I was driving on State Street, still relatively close to the dojo, and the damn lion started to shit right in the car," Gregory said. "I had a magazine in the car, so I slapped it behind me, right in the back seat, right in the pile she just made, and she covered the damn magazine. The red light changed to green, but I didn't care. I opened the door, got out, tossed the magazine on the ground and drove away. It smelled so damn bad."

Floyd Webb met someone during his research for *Search for Count Dante* who was bitten by the lion on one of the Chicago beaches.

Because she tore up his apartment, Keehan took to keeping Aurelia at one of his dojos. In an interview with Webb, Robert C. Brown said that when the lion was about one and a half years old, she would walk out into the practicing area while students were training. "She'd come up behind you and sweep your feet out. We learned the art of foot sweeps from that lion," he joked.

Bob Wall also encountered Keehan one day while he was out for a stroll with Aurelia. At the time he didn't know Keehan, but his companion did. "What a sight. He was a muscular guy. He wasn't a giant, but he was a tough-looking guy. You just figured he was strapped and dangerous."

Keehan sold his pet to a businessman from Quincy, Illinois, after his landlord put his foot down. In October 1964, the lion was taken to a Lions Club event in Quincy. She bit the town's mayor while he tried to get her to pose for a photo op, according to the *Chicago Tribune*.

A few days after the lion was handed over to her new owner, the buyer called Keehan's dojo.

" 'You guys come and pick this son of a bitch up! He bit me and I'm bleeding all over the place!' " Gregory recalled the owner saying.

"We just hung up."

1964 WORLD KARATE TOURNAMENT

In 1964 Keehan put on his second USKA World Karate Tournament at the Chicago Coliseum. His goal was to make it grander in every way possible than the previous year's.

On the morning of the first day, Floyd Webb ran through the aisles of chairs at the Coliseum, past women in beehives, wise guys in cheap suits, and others gathered to see a martial arts tournament.

Webb was hanging around with friends Luther and Mike. All three were about eleven years old, Black, and used to getting kicked out of places whether they were causing trouble or not. The only places they ever felt welcome were at museums. On the way to those museums, they would pass by the Chicago Coliseum. The structure was once used as a prisoner of war camp during the Civil War.

Webb grew up in the Harold L. Ickes Homes, three blocks east of Chinatown. He and his friends would pick up odd jobs in Chinatown, like cleaning nasty galvanized aluminum garbage cans at the restaurants. Or they would sell copies of the *Chicago Defender* and *Jet* magazines. They did anything they could do to make some extra money, mainly for comic books. They were already fascinated with martial arts through Bruce Tegner books they'd pick up at a mobile library. The nearest full library was in the Loop and too far away. Tegner was the only martial arts author the mobile library carried. So when they saw posters up around Chinatown for the 1964 US Karate Association's World Karate Tournament at the Coliseum, they went for it.

"We bought our tickets for $2, and inside this place it looked more like a big wrestling event or a fight card than any karate event we'd seen," Webb said.

There were about three thousand people at the venue on Wabash Avenue south of the Loop.

It was a mixed crowd, evenly Black and white. Webb remembers being surprised at the ratio. You didn't usually see this much racial mixing in public, at least not in his experience. Many in the crowd were dressed to the nines, some of them carrying decks of cards, taken as a sign of affiliation with the Chicago Outfit. Amid the din, people milled about, socialized, and reacted to the different fights and demonstrations.

Webb and crew kept moving around to the different exhibitions. They saw Tigi Mataalii try to shatter a large ice chunk; a group from the Philippines, using sticks and knives, demonstrated a form unknown to Webb and his friends. There were even women demonstrating fighting forms. And they were thrilled to see Ray Cooper, one of the few Black black belts at the time. Cooper fought against Mike Stone and seemed to have won the combat portion of the tournament, though the decision went to Stone.

The boys wandered through the arena until they came across a striking man with red hair and a goatee. He was wearing an expensive-looking sport coat and slacks. He was appealing and scary all at once.

"What are you kids doing?" Keehan asked.

"Please don't kick us out," Webb recalled saying.

"Come and sit over here."

The boys, stunned silent, followed the man to the main ring. He directed them to a trio of front row seats, right on the floor.

"I want you guys down in front so you can see the matches better," Keehan said.

"We really thought he was going to kick us out," Webb recollected. "We had been kicked out of seedier places than that. We had seen Keehan being mean and mouthing off to people. But he was really nice to us. I couldn't believe it. No white man in his position was *ever* that nice to us."

The fighting was raw and scary and yet attractive, like Keehan himself. Webb could see teeth fly across the mats during a match. A group of Muslims faced off against a team of marines. It turned into a massive brawl and spilled out onto the street outside of the Coliseum.

Later, after the tournament, young Webb was so intrigued he decided to call Keehan directly and ask him about training at his school at Eighty-First Street and Ashland Avenue. When Webb told him his age, Keehan insisted that he speak to Webb's mother.

Webb's mother got on the phone with him and after their talk, she decided not to allow him to enroll.

"I had to go through some real dangerous white neighborhoods to get to where he was," Webb said.

Webb looked elsewhere for martial arts instruction, finding it with classmates Clarence and Marshall Jordan. The two were studying under Gregory Jaco, a Vietnam veteran who opened dojos on Chicago's South Side after returning from the war.

Jaco, who is the father of rapper Lupe Fiasco and dancer/choreographer Ayesha Jaco, found solace in martial arts while growing up. He wanted to create alternatives to gang life and other crime paths just like martial arts provided for him as a kid. In the 1970s, he opened the Tornado School of Martial Arts.

"Jaco didn't charge his students," Webb said. "People and parents could make donations. Jaco was really concerned with grades, always checking to see how you were doing in school. He always wanted kids to have more than he did."

Jaco's dojo didn't have the glitz of Keehan's. Jaco set up wherever he could find an affordable space, often in storefronts. Because he didn't charge his students, Jaco's operation depended upon donations to pay for space, uniforms, and equipment.

Despite their simple facilities, Jaco's students were tough and well trained. The brothers were extreme in their own training as well and expected that of Webb. One day, they called Webb and asked him to join them in an outside workout. It was ten degrees below zero.

"I had been reading about Mas Oyama training out in the snow and waterfalls, so I figured I could try," Webb said. "We got out in the snow and worked out for about an hour. Once you get moving you're hot."

Webb was also part of a Boy Scouts of America Explorer post, which included other Jaco students and focused on martial arts.

When Webb brought up Keehan to his new sensei, Jaco warned him off.

"Jaco, as my first sensei, knew my interest in Keehan. He told me many times to stay away," Webb said. "He thought Keehan was straight-up crazy. He once told me, 'Sooner or later, someone's going to die because of him or something crazy he's doing.'"

THE FALLOUT WITH TRIAS

After the 1964 tournament, Keehan seemed to be on a roll. Scores of eager students flocked to classes at his dojos, many of them Black.

Promoted to head instructor of the USKA, Keehan was lauded as being one of the top karate instructors in the United States by *Black Belt*. Keehan was running two schools in 1964, the Imperial Academy of Fighting Arts on Rush Street and another dojo at 7902 North Ashland Avenue.

But soon Keehan was removed from the organization Trias had founded under a heavy cloud of speculation. In an interview with *Black Belt*, Keehan alleged that that the split with USKA was prompted by Trias's "prejudicial bias" against his African American students.

"It's no secret that I have a great many blacks in my school," the fighter reported to *Black Belt*. "That was the reason behind my rift with Robert Trias and the USKA. At that time, the USKA didn't have any blacks in the organization, except mine, and Trias didn't like that one bit. He even told me that I had promoted the second black in his organization. And, according to him, the first was by mistake. He told me that he slipped . . . the USKA did not award black belts to blacks."

In a letter dated December 7, 1964, Keehan was formally barred from the USKA that he had done so much to promote.

According to *Black Belt*, a letter confirming Keehan's removal read, "Please be advised that Mr. John Keehan has been expelled from the organization for various violations against the constitution of the USKA under article XI-V, and for conduct unbecoming the true spirit of karate-do . . . let us not at any time support those who seek to weaken and undermine the true Karate way."

Trias told Ayoob that Keehan "had a lot of good ideas about promoting the tournaments and other karate activities, but some of his ideas were so fantastically out of reason."

Trias also complained that Keehan routinely lied about his past military service and other elements of his personal history. "He'd print stuff about having been here, having been there, having been with Castro, just fantastic stories that were really hurting the organization," Trias was quoted as saying.

Tommy Gregory remembered that Keehan and Trias once had an argument after Keehan made the fanciful claim, in a brochure to promote the 1964 tournament, that Trias once fought a bear.

"Apparently, (Keehan) listened to the wrong people, got a little power hungry," Trias told Ayoob. "He did a lot of good for the organization when he was with it. He was well liked."

Robert Bartkowski, a Chicago-area kung fu instructor, said the Trias/Keehan split, "had just as much to do with a personality clash. Everything Keehan did, he probably overdid. I think he had a lot of good ideas at the time. They were a little radical. I think the combination of his personality and his flamboyance doesn't take away the validity of what he was trying to do."

Keehan himself said the split had come expressly because he was promoting Black students to black belt, something that was "tacitly forbidden" by the USKA.

Keehan student Michael Felkoff said, in an interview with Webb, that Trias was "up front with Keehan about his displeasure with promoting Black people to black belt/shodan."

Keehan continued training students at his schools and formed the World Karate Federation to put on tournaments. He lost several talented students and tournament winners who chose to stick with Trias and the USKA, but he still had a solid roster of instructors, including Jim Koncevic and Doug Dwyer. Edgell stuck with Keehan as well, eventually teaching aikido to Keehan's students.

While his removal from Trias's USKA was a setback, it freed Keehan to bring his more extreme martial arts ideas to life, a portent of today's MMA-dominated fighting sports scene.

KARATE DOESN'T WORK IN A PHONE BOOTH OR A PRISON CELL: ARTHUR RAPKIN'S STORY

In late 1964, when he was sixteen, Arthur Rapkin left his home and his hometown of Milwaukee, driving away in his Chevy Bel Air sedan. He was headed to Chicago.

His mission: find John Keehan.

As a kid, Rapkin had always felt out of place. He grew up an overweight, unathletic Jewish kid who was always picked last in gym class. In tenth grade he was expelled from high school. Then he was kicked out of his karate class. It hadn't helped his life on either front that he'd gotten into an actual street fight with a teacher from his high school who also was a student at the karate school.

"The head of the school was a Polish guy who studied Okinawan karate while there in the marines," Rapkin said, the memory still fresh fifty-seven years later. "His whole thing was very traditional. You'd go through the motions. Bowing, forms, no contact. No contact! You're studying this method of fighting but you don't want to fight because you could hurt someone. How does that prepare you if someone's trying to hurt you?

"There was much bullshit in karate then. It was so fake. Just 'Let's pretend to be Asian.'"

So it was that Rapkin went looking for Keehan.

"I did my research on where to train next and under whom," he said. "Either I could go to Japan, Thailand, or Burma, or I could find this master that was known throughout the United States, and he was in Chicago."

At the time, Keehan was still rebuilding after his split with Trias and he needed new blood to build up the World Karate Federation, especially since powerful students like Jimmy Jones stayed with Trias's USKA.

When Rapkin arrived at Keehan's dojo above Mister Kelly's on Rush Street, he was not disappointed. Mister Kelly's was a famous Chicago nightclub which existed from 1953 to 1975. Over the years, headliners included Woody Allen, Lenny Bruce, Flip Wilson, Bill Cosby, George Carlin, Richard Pryor, Eartha Kitt, Joan Rivers, Aretha Franklin, Liza Minnelli, Barbra Streisand, Ella Fitzgerald, and Billie Holiday.

"It was a supernova in the local and national nightlife firmament," according to an article in the *Chicago Tribune*.

And right upstairs . . . John Keehan.

"I was pretty impressed with the place, the guy, everything about him. His build, his stature, his way of carrying himself. He was awe-inspiring. It was like everything I had read and heard about him was apparently true."

There was only one problem. After putting Rapkin through his paces, Keehan told the youngster he wasn't quite ready to play with the big boys.

"Because I wasn't a black belt he wouldn't take me as a student."

Instead, Keehan sent him to a dojo run by his student, Jim Koncevic.

Koncevic was a formidable figure, larger even than Dante at six feet three inches and 250 pounds. Koncevic had been one of Keehan's first students. Now he ran the Tai-Jutsu School of Judo and Karate at 3030 North Central Avenue on the west side. Like his master, his instruction style tended toward brutal and realistic.

In time, Koncevic would become a decorated judo competitor who later turned to karate and became a serious force in karate competitions as well. *Black Belt* listed him in January 1965 taking first place as a white belt in karate, sparring at the fifth annual Midwest Karate Championship. Later, in 1969, *Black Belt* described two decisive victories by Koncevic in a tournament, noting his speed and force but also his honed precision with punches and kicks alike.

Also like his master, Koncevic loved a fight—a brawler who didn't hesitate to use his full arsenal on the streets when challenged. He didn't look for fights, but he never backed down from them either. He was dog-loyal to Keehan; his sensei could do no wrong. He was always down for whatever, ready to stand elbow to elbow if needed.

And for his loyalty, Koncevic would eventually pay the ultimate price.

Both Keehan's and Koncevic's classes reflected their attitude about martial arts. Keehan's mantra: street fights take place in the streets.

Competitive athletes know they need to train under realistic conditions to excel. With that in mind, students were not babied. In the early days, when the dojo didn't have mats yet, students would grapple on concrete floors. Part of a class would consist of step-by-step drills of karate and judo techniques; the rest of the time would be real-time full contact. As Rapkin understood, Keehan's teachings were a cross-discipline mixture of aikido, karate, and judo.

Rapkin, still in his teens, was one of the youngest students. From what he remembers, the other students were at the youngest in their early twenties and up to the late thirties on the older end. They were all bigger than him, more manly in every way. They had adult jobs—police officers, construction workers. Some were gang members. Several were older, with families.

Rapkin said that students would generally be paired up, one holding a large kicking pad while the other would kick repeatedly, and then they'd switch. Sometimes they would practice self-defense scenarios where one would come at the other with a knife or a gun and the unarmed would have to disarm their mock assailant.

"We got hurt a lot. I didn't like getting hurt like that at first. You had to either become more aggressive than the other guy or be really good defensively. But if you could make it through a class with Koncevic, you could hold your own in all sorts of situations."

Rapkin spent the next eight months training under Koncevic before he earned a brown belt in karate. At times, Koncevic would bring his students to Keehan's school on Ashland Avenue. Keehan could see that Rapkin was a fast learner.

Because he was so loyal and committed, Rapkin was allowed to join Keehan's classes after earning his brown belt.

Rapkin became a fixture in the dojo. He stuck around after classes, eager to learn more from the master; Keehan, in turn, began mentoring the kid in and out of the dojo.

Rapkin even earned a nickname among the other Keehan disciples, who called him "Rapkindo." In part it was a joke, but it was also an acknowledgement of his toughness. In time Rapkindo began sleeping at the dojo, in the back room, not far from the lion in her cage.

Keehan believed that the mind could be trained to embrace transformation. He would have Rapkin and other students sit legs folded in front of a mirror and go into a deep meditation where they would envision themselves as a tiger or another fierce animal. He encouraged them to make faces with wild eyes and scowls to intimidate their future opponents.

" 'You have to put yourself in a tiger mindset,' he would tell us," Rapkin said. "You have to *explode*. If you're going to fight, you don't want to fight from a human mentality. You want to fight from an animal mentality. And you don't want to wait to react.

"Martial arts were invented to protect farmers from wild animals. If you're going to have to defend yourself against a wild animal, then you have to be like a wild animal, he would say."

Of course, Rapkin's favorite Keehanism was this: "Karate isn't effective in a phone booth."

"I'll never forget him saying that to me," Rapkin said. "And you know what? I've experienced it in real life and he's right. Karate isn't effective in a prison cell either."

Keehan's dojo above Mr. Kelley's had bright fluorescent lights hanging from the ceiling and mirrors along the walls. A single red 25-watt lightbulb hung in a corner with no fixture.

The whole time he'd been working out there, Rapkin often wondered what the red light was for. One night during class, he found out.

Keehan positioned Rapkin under the red light. Then he positioned six men around Rapkin, some armed with weapons. Then he turned off the fluorescents, leaving only the dim red bulb—a classroom simulation of a night fight with multiple attackers.

"You ready?" Keehan asked?

"No?" Rapkin ventured, unsure.

With a half grin, Keehan walked over to Rapkin and said "Listen: Just take 'em out one at a time. Start with the one who is closest. Then go to next guy, the next guy, the next guy. One at a time, right? That's all. One at a time."

Rapkin still looked uncertain.

"Remember: tiger mind," Keehan said. "You must have the mind of a tiger. Put your mind into your breath. Put your breath into your mind. Initiate the fight. Take it to them one at a time. And make the first move very stunning. You have to stun your opponents, especially when there's more than one. Make each blow count."

Rapkin took a moment to delve into his animal state, just like Keehan taught him, and waded into the fray.

As time went on, Keehan became fond of Rapkin. Knowing the kid needed a way to support himself, Keehan encouraged him to become a hairdresser. "If you can land anywhere with scissors, you'll always be able to meet women and make a living," Keehan told him.

Keehan also showed him how, if he was ballsy enough, he could play by his own rules.

One day, in the middle of one of their typical conversations, Rapkin said hopefully, "John, I want to open my own karate school."

"Then open a school," Keehan said.

"Well, I need to be a black belt first, don't I?"

"You don't need to be a black belt. There's no law that you need one to open a karate school. Just open one. You'll teach people what you know. What do they know about karate? They don't know nothing."

Incredibly enough, within the space of two years, the eighteen-year-old Rapkin opened the Wisconsin Institute of Self Defense, six blocks from his former high school.

"The opening was like a zoo," Rapkin recalled. "I had local police, even gym teachers from the high school there. I did it. And it was a really cool school, if I do say so myself."

BLASTING CAPS

Over time, Keehan would become infamous for his self-destructive acts. As quick as he built his reputation of legit accomplishments in martial arts, his outrageous behavior would earn him scorn. His push to be uncommon would lead to danger, starting with the time in the summer of 1965 when he tried to blow out the windows at a Chicago dojo. He had been an instructor there before joining up with Trias and then opening his own school.

On July 23, 1965, according to an article in the *Chicago Tribune*, Keehan and his associate, Doug Dwyer, were questioned "about a detonating cap and a length of wire found taped to the front door of the Chicago Judo and Karate Center" at 4222 South Archer Avenue.

The men were seized after a high-speed chase with police. During the chase, a box containing thirteen more dynamite blasting caps was thrown from the car.

According to the article, the men were suspected of going to the rival dojo with the intention of blowing out the windows. Keehan claimed the operator of the dojo, Gene Wyka, owed them money for class instruction both men had given at his school.

According to the article, the CJK dojo was spared because Keehan and Dwyer had been drinking heavily and were unable to set fire to the fuse.

Later, in an interview with Ayoob for *Black Belt*, Keehan said that he had a falling out with Wyka.

The plan, as Keehan described it to Ayoob, was to "tape the dynamite caps to the window, light the fuse, take off, and we'd go around the block, but when we came around again it hadn't gone. The fuse was just sittin' there. It was falling off the window. After three or four times—this was basically a shopping area in Chicago, and there was no business at night, this was like two in the morning—the police finally spotted us."

Earlier that month, according to the *Tribune*, there had been four similar bombings in the Loop area of Chicago. State Rep. Robert R. Canfield, at the time a member of a state commission charged with investigating the bombings and their connection to the Chicago Outfit, told the *Tribune:* "All bombings of this type are intimidation, and these are intended to achieve a goal."

Police were on high alert for anything bombing-related when they found Keehan and Dwyer near Wyka's school.

According to the *Tribune*, Keehan and Dwyer were subjected to lie detector tests and asked, among other questions, if they were members of the Chicago Outfit. Authorities would later say they believed the pair's activities were not connected to the other bombings.

According to Keehan's FBI report, Keehan told Chicago police that because of the recent hubbub about the bombings, he and Dwyer had intended to throw the blasting caps into Lake Michigan. But then, in order to "to blow off a little steam," Keehan said he decided to place one of the caps on Wyka's window.

Keehan was charged with attempted arson and possession of explosives. Dwyer was charged with four traffic violations. Also, both were charged with possession of explosives and resisting arrest and were sentenced in October 1965 to two years of probation.

What exactly led to Wyka and Keehan falling out is not clear. AlGene Caraulia's take is that Wyka's traditional integrity and Keehan's blasé big-talking didn't mesh. Keehan also would leave for months at a time to train with Trias in Arizona.

"I have a feeling that Keehan's problem with Gene is that our organization was successful," Caraulia said. "We were making a profit just through the schools, and John wasn't. All of his talk about how good he was, but he didn't know how to make an income from teaching martial arts."

Caraulia noted that Keehan likely chose the location on Forty-Second and Archer because it was on the ground floor. Incidentally, the window Keehan tried to blow out housed Caraulia's various competition trophies—including Caraulia's trophy from the 1963 tournament.

"Why attack the window when you can attack the person?" Caraulia mused. "A martial arts fight is supposed to be between people, not glass. I had a real laugh over it when I read about it in the news."

An FBI report dated November 29, 1965, started with a synopsis on Keehan that ended with an all caps and underlined warning that mirrored the US Army's assessment of him five years earlier:

<u>KEEHAN SHOULD BE CONSIDERED DANGEROUS BECAUSE HE REPORTEDLY IS SUBJECT TO A VIOLENT AND ANTI-SOCIAL BEHAVIOR PATTERN AND HAS SUICIDAL TENDENCIES</u>.

RAPKIN VS. THE BULL

In the summer of 1967, Keehan and Rapkin were hanging out at the dojo after hours. They'd been laughing and talking shit, but then, suddenly, Keehan became quiet. He looked at Rapkin intently.

"I'm granting you an opportunity to do something amazing and special," he told his dedicated pupil, who was by now just shy of twenty.

Rapkin's dojo back in Milwaukee was doing well. There was nothing he wouldn't do for his sensei.

Keehan began telling him about Sosai Matsutatu Oyama, a renowned karate master who founded Kyokushin Karate. Oyama was always searching for unique ways to push the limits of his martial arts skills. In 1950, after spending eighteen months training alone in the mountains of Japan, he decided to fight bulls. Over time, Oyama would tour Japan, Mexico, the United States, and other countries taking on bulls in front of spectators.

The fights were not the traditional, Spanish kind, with the matador and the twirling cape. In these fights, the muscular Oyama would appear before a crowd in a field, barehanded, wearing only sparring shorts and a tight wide band around his waist.

Taking the bull by the horns, like a rodeo cowboy, he'd grapple it to the ground. In one old film, a strong punch knocks one horn off the beast.

As it happened, Keehan was planning to put on a tournament. "Wouldn't this be a great way to publicize the event?" Keehan told the kid. "I'll bet if that guy Oyama could do it, you could, too."

Rapkin looked at him, stunned. Later he'd say, "Being a young guy under John Keehan and getting this chance, man! It felt like Elvis Presley telling you to sing 'That's Alright Mama' with him in Sun Studios."

In an era long before the Internet made looking up old film clips a snap, Keehan assured Rapkin that the Japanese bulls Oyama fought were the size of large Great Danes or small ponies (not the actual case).

The next day, Keehan called Rapkin to meet him on State Street. A flatbed truck pulled up with a two-thousand-pound Brahman bull tied to the railing along the rear bed. Rapkin pulled himself up into the truck bed next to the bull and a fellow Keehan student bellowed into a megaphone:

"Come to the Medinah Temple and see this brave young karate expert take on this ferocious bull!"

They drove up and down State Street for the next couple hours. Someone even called the TV news.

"This wasn't too many years after my bar mitzvah," Rapkin said. "I'm with these maniacs in Chicago, and I'm this little, overweight Jewish kid from Milwaukee who wasn't good at sports, but who wanted to be a tough guy."

Though admittedly a little afraid—he'd been in the truck all day with the massive bull, doing his best to keep his distance—Rapkin set about training. It was routine for him to spar with bigger guys. He could break bricks—two bricks, three bricks at a time. He started telling himself, "How hard can it be to fight a bull? Oyama did it."

On September 14, 1967, nineteen-year-old Rapkin entered the Medinah Temple as scheduled. The historic auditorium, located in Near North Chicago, was built in a Moorish revival style, replete with the characteristic pointed domes and mosaics.

As people streamed into the auditorium, Rapkin went through his warm-up routine. Ever since Keehan told him he would fight the bull, he really believed it would happen. He believed every time he trained that he would have face the beast with nothing to defend him but his two hands.

The cops showed up with an order to shut down the show. Tickets were not refunded.

Asked what they planned to do with the bull since they couldn't fight it, Rapkin told the *Chicago Tribune* he would "kill it in the truck in State Street if necessary."

About a year later, the *Tribune* was writing about the duo again.

According to an article published on September 9, 1968, police were investigating the theft of $8,600 in gate receipts from the World Karate Federation tournament held at the Chicago Coliseum.

According to the article, Rapkin was listed as treasurer of the federation. He told police that after he placed the money inside a truck in the Coliseum parking lot, he'd gone to make a phone call. Another man named Roy Rose, who also was watching the truck, was paged on a public address system. "When they returned the money was gone," according to the *Tribune*."

In the reporting for this book, Rapkin said that Keehan had instructed him to steal the money and then notify the police. Apparently police did not explore this option. According to Freedom of Information requests, the Chicago Police Department has no records of this incident in relation to Rapkin or Keehan.

By 1967, Edgell had earned his black belt, moved on from Keehan's dojo, and gained a strong reputation in the Chicago area as a martial arts instructor. Looking to open a new location for his Imperial Academy of Fighting Arts, Keehan asked Edgell to come back and teach.

Edgell was content with his current situation. He was doing well on his own. He didn't want to teach more classes.

Keehan insisted. "He said, 'Woody, would you please come down to my school? I'll make you an offer you won't be able to refuse.' I will never forget that," Edgell said.

Edgell met Keehan at the school, and despite Keehan's persistence, he still wasn't persuaded to join.

Keehan suggested they take a drive. They were joined by a few of Keehan's teachers and ended up in "a dumpy looking bar somewhere on the South Side," Edgell said. They went inside, grabbed drinks from the bar, and sat down at a table to talk. The bar was barely half full and dimly lit.

Mid-conversation, Edgell noticed a large man approaching the table with a quickness that likely meant he wasn't interested in making pleasantries.

"This guy must've weighed three hundred pounds and he wasn't fat," Edgell said. "He grabbed me around my chest and threw me across the room. I landed on a table, which luckily broke my fall. I'm like 'what the hell is going on?' "

The attacker cussed him out as he marched over to Edgell's landing spot, as Edgell was shaking off wood splinters and trying to get a grip on the situation. He reached down to grab Edgell, but Edgell's training kicked in.

"I grabbed him by the throat and jabbed both of his eyeballs, and he started screaming," Edgell said.

Keehan and his crew quickly came over and broke up the fight.

As Edgell caught his breath, he noticed they were all laughing—even Keehan.

"John glanced up at the bartender and said, 'Send me the bill,' " Edgell said. "Here I am thinking this guy's trying to kill me and then they're all laughing about it like it's no big deal."

Edgell, Keehan and the other teachers left the bar and drove north back to the dojo.

En route, Edgell demanded to know "what the fuck had just happened."

"You passed the test," Keehan said.

"*What?*" Edgell asked.

"When I promoted you to second degree black belt, some of the guys at the dojo were upset about it. They felt like they didn't know what you could really do. Even though I reminded them that in my dojo, I am the one who decides if people get promoted, they were *still* complaining. So I thought I'd let you show them yourself."

Edgell was pissed at the manipulation, but he was also kind of touched at Keehan's confidence in him.

About thirty years later, Edgell ran into one of the fellow instructors from Keehan's schools. The two reminisced on the old days, and Edgell brought up Keehan's test at the bar.

"He told me I wasn't the first or the last person to take that test. I couldn't believe it. He knew at least a dozen people who went through it."

COUNT DANTE AND THE WORLD'S DEADLIEST FIGHTING SECRETS

Around 1965, Keehan was "was fed up with karate and a lot of the bad things that were happening to him in karate," Edgell said. "He decided he wanted to change his style completely."

He began studying under a Chinese master named James Lee.

Lee had learned his martial arts when he lived as a monk at a Shaolin temple. He was respectful of his art and picky about whom he taught.

Soon after Keehan began training with Lee, Edgell was offered the opportunity as well.

"It was the hardest training I ever did," Edgell said. "They beat the living shit out of me."

According to Edgell, Lee's martial arts system included a fabled martial arts technique called *Dim Mak*. Translated, it means "touch of death."

While Lee may well have taught Dim Mak to Keehan and Edgell, there is no evidence that such a martial arts unicorn has ever actually existed.

The concept of the touch of death traces its history to traditional Chinese acupuncture. Apparently, Dim Mak uses pressure points and meridians said to incapacitate or sometimes cause immediate or even delayed death to an opponent. Tales of its use are often found in Chinese martial arts fiction. Some have claimed Bruce Lee was killed by a delayed reaction to a Dim Mak strike, among other mythic takes on what caused his mysterious death.

In 1967, Keehan changed his name legally to Count Juan Raphael Dante. He claimed it was his rightful name as a descendant of Spanish royalty.

Edgell never called Keehan by his new name, nor did any of the people who originally knew him as John Keehan, Edgell said. "He told me the name change was an act of showmanship," Edgell said. "He realized that if he became like a heel in pro wrestling, a villain of sorts, he'd be more memorable."

Looking back, it seems obvious that he was a man constantly in transition, ever morphing and reinventing, adding pieces learned from mentors, like any good student, and making it his own.

He'd already begun dying his red hair black and permed it into an Afro-style hairdo. Then he began sculpting his beard with depilatory powder, making precise curves and swoops and sharp points reminiscent of the noted Satanist Anton Szandor LaVey. The process took a lot of time in front of a mirror, but he was a skilled beautician after all. Delicately he would apply the powder a little at a time, then wipe it off to form the shapes. The astringent nature of the hair remover caused his cheeks and chin to appear chapped and raw. Soon after, he began wearing the dark Dracula-style cape with a colorful lining and carrying a 24-carat gold embossed walking stick. Completing the outfit, he often wore dancers' leotards.

"He wasn't a normal person. He wanted attention," Rapkin said. "And the more attention he got, it still wasn't enough. It was never enough. He looked like Bruce Lee and Prince rolled into one."

In 1968, the newly named Count Dante released the three pamphlets that would make him a worldwide celebrity.

Titled *World's Deadliest Fighting Secrets* and advertised in Marvel and other comic books with now-iconic ads featuring the Count, the pamphlets were available for free (plus twenty-five cents postage) by mail order, in the style of the day.

Central to his deadly fighting secrets was Dim Mak, the touch of death.

"On that pulse-pounding ad page," wrote Chicago writer and Dante enthusiast Paco Taylor, "Dante loomed as a badass karate master. Garbed in a black martial arts gi, the fighter's chiseled arms slithered menacingly from dark nothingness. His fighting stance was punctuated with fierce, fang-like fingers coiled tightly into the dreaded *Dim Mak* (death touch). Empty eyes bled down from sharply arched eyebrows, and a black beard, edged sideburns, and a pointed widow's peak ascended into the rounded crown of a faux Afro."

One of his ads touted his badass reputation:

Count Danté is the undefeated Supreme Grand Master of the Fighting Arts. Count Danté on the World Overall Fighting Arts Championship (Master & Expert Divisions) after defeating the world top Masters of JUDO, BOXING, WRESTLING, KUNG-FU, KARATE, AKIDO, etc. in Death Matches. On August 1, 1967, the World Federation of Fighting Arts crowned the Count "THE WORLD'S DEADLIEST FIGHTING ARTS CHAMPION AND MASTER."

Another ad concentrated on the technique:

Yes, this is the DEADLIEST and most TERRIFYING fighting art known to man—and WITHOUT EQUAL. Its MAIMING, MUTILATING, DISFIGURING, PARALYZING, and CRIPPLING techniques are known by only a few people in the world. An expert at DIM MAK could easily kill many Judo, Karate, Kung Fu, Aikido, and Gung Fu experts at one time with only finger-tip pressure using his murderous POISON HAND WEAPONS. Instructing you step by step thru each move in this manual is none other than COUNT DANTE— "THE DEADLIEST MAN WHO EVER LIVED." (THE CROWN PRINCE OF DEATH.)

Inside the pamphlets, which arrived faithfully because of a mail order operation that contracted for the services of a local nunnery, correspondents were rewarded with depictions of such techniques as the "Poison Hands." The pamphlets also advertised Black Dragon Fighting Society swag for sale, including a line of sweatshirts, sweatpants, nunchucks, warm-up jackets, acrylic yawara sticks, shuriken, and other gear inscribed with the Black Dragon Fighting Society logo.

After the pamphlet was released, according to Edgell, Lee and Dante fell out.

According to Edgell, Lee feared retribution if it was ever discovered that he'd taught Dante Dim Mak.

James Lee could not be located for this story.

In the late 1960s, seeking to increase his empire in Chicago, Dante took ownership of several adult and occult bookstores. Marc Lully also had a stake in the bookstores, and he knew a man named Michael Bertiaux, a social worker, writer, and artist who was said to have extensive knowledge of Haitian voodoo.

Bertiaux's counseling work at the time focused on Haitian immigrants, and he practiced for almost forty years. In Bertiaux, Dante saw optimism and an open mind. He wanted to learn how to tap into those kinds of spiritual powers.

In early 1970, Bertiaux invited Dante to his apartment at 5120 South Hyde Park Avenue. Dante arrived at around 4 p.m. on a Wednesday, dressed in dark slacks and a sweater, carrying a small, blue crystal ball. The two sat at a small table in Bertiaux's home with a white linen tablecloth draped over it. Atop the table sat two candlesticks, a stand to burn sandalwood incense, and the crystal ball that Dante brought, Bertiaux said.

"It's a ritual to begin our association with the spirits as a teacher and pupil," Bertiaux said. "We set up in the middle of the room with him facing me. We had quiet periods similar to meditation, and we also just talked."

The first session lasted less than an hour.

"Dante believed everyone had a potential to become a superhero," Bertiaux said. "He didn't believe that circumstances were permanent limitations. He was working with inner city kids that were held back economically and socially, and he wanted to inspire optimism. He was a terrific optimist who believed nothing could hold a person back from succeeding or ascending in some way. They just needed to make up their mind to do it."

Bertiaux advised Dante on ways to encourage people who were on the verge of giving up, such as pointing out incremental progress.

Dante wasn't trying to foist voodoo practices on his students. Instead, he was trying to deepen his own spirituality to help his students' find more inner strength, Bertiaux said.

"He felt he was going to change things," Bertiaux said. "He had that confidence."

They continued meeting, usually weekly, for about the next two years, Bertiaux said. After a few months of regularly meeting, Dante asked Bertiaux a question about identity.

"He said to me 'my birth name is John Keehan, but I like this name Count Dante,' " Bertiaux said.

"I told him that when people play a role, the role becomes them and transforms them. So I said: 'If you feel you can bear and sustain what you expect to be the energies of Count Dante, use it. If you feel that it's overwhelming and too powerful, go back to being John Keehan.' "

Dante never brought it up again.

ENTER THE DRAGON LADY

Carrie Anders was fourteen years old when she first met John Keehan. Keehan's father was friends with Anders's father; the two would often sail together on the Keehans' boat. Carrie and John would frequently join them out on Lake Michigan, she said.

"I had a huge crush on him even then," Anders said in an interview. As of 2021, she was seventy-six.

The crush continued through high school, but Keehan was always Keehan. After promising to be her date to the senior prom, he stood her up. Anders didn't hear from Keehan again until about five years after high school, in 1967.

At the time, she was working at the Playboy Club in Chicago, serving drinks and cigarettes while dressed in a form-fitting, high-waisted bunny costume, with bunny ears atop her head and a poofy tail on her ass. After a failed relationship, Anders was living with her parents and raising her son as a single mom.

"I was staying with my folks while I figured out my next move," said Anders, whose surname has been changed at her request.

One day after a shift at the club, Anders came home to find a dozen red roses waiting for her. A note, written in gold ink on black stationery, was signed "Count Dante."

"The note said something to the effect of: 'The burning embers of love can be rekindled.' And I thought: 'Who the hell is this? How did I set a fire in someone's heart?'"

Shortly after that, she came home after a shift and found a message on her answering machine from a photographer. Unbeknownst to her, photos had been taken while she modeled at a recent Chicago auto show.

She called the number given. Someone picked up the phone and said, "This is John Keehan."

By this time, Keehan was well into his Dante transformation, and his chocolate-brown Cadillac Eldorado convertible had emblazoned on its front doors a family crest he created as part of his Dante identity.

Dante wasted no time in getting to the reason for contacting Anders: he wanted to rekindle their relationship.

"If you've ever been jilted," Anders said, a bilious tone rising in her voice, even after all these years, "you know how you *fantasize* about seeing that person again? You think: what would I say to this horrible person who did this to me?"

"He just kept saying it over and over: 'Please just let me see you,' " Anders recalled.

"I kept saying 'no' *repeatedly*."

Finally, Anders relented, on the condition they spend only a short time together.

Dante drove to her folks' house in the brown Caddy. She met him at the curb. No sooner had she settled into the front seat to talk—imagining they'd sit a spell in front of the house, as people would often do back then—Dante took off.

He drove around their old neighborhood, going nowhere in particular, mostly around the streets where they'd grown up. Dante seemed nostalgic for the old days, but he was also grandiose, regaling her with his life plans. He made sure to apologize for standing her up at the prom—he had plans for that, too, ways and more ways to make it up to her, he promised.

Apparently moved by his earnestness, and maybe just a bit by the promise of this wonderful life he claimed to be having, Anders agreed to stop for a drink at a bar near Seventy-Ninth Street near South Shore Drive. A nearby motel offered hourly rates; he may have visited a time or two in the past. But she was determined to hold her ground, to investigate, to only have one drink with John, or Dante, or whatever he was calling himself now.

Meanwhile, back at Anders's parents' house, Anders's steady boyfriend showed up. Her parents didn't know where she was. Everyone grew concerned.

When Anders breezed in the front door some hours later, the boyfriend was full of questions. Anders deflected, telling him she'd been out with this guy Dante, a hairdresser she knew from the Playboy Club—which was not entirely a lie.

But the boyfriend remained suspicious. Anders was no Mata Hari; she was a struggling single mom doing the best she could. Finally, she started to cry.

"'That was the boy who broke my heart,'" she explained.

From there, the rekindled relationship grew. The attraction between Dante and Anders was unmistakable. The pull of the years was strong. He was strong and attractive, if not a little overproduced with the jet-black hair and the sculpted beard. Still, compared with the saps and nimrods always vying for her attention at the club, Dante was a breath of fresh hair. He was a dreamer. He was creative. And he was just dangerous enough to make him intriguing.

"One thing led to another, and I ended up living with him," Anders said.

In time, Anders became fully swept up in Dante's world. She quit the Playboy Club and Dante put her on at the Imperial Academy of Fighting Arts, where she enrolled new students, did promotional work, and lent a hand wherever needed around the dojo.

Anders also took up karate, with Dante giving her private lessons. Surprised and impressed by her toughness, he nicknamed her the Dragon Lady. She accompanied him everywhere, day and night. They became inseparable.

"He was a very charismatic guy, but he had a dark side and a controlling side. It was not long before he had pretty much control of my mind," Anders said.

It was Anders who helped Dante plan the big tournament in September 1967—the one where Arthur Rapkin thought he would fight a bull. The bullfight's shock pageantry was to fill the seats. Once people were at the event, seated and attentive, the big audience would be exposed to Dante's full-contact vision of martial arts. That's one way Dante kept telling Anders that he'd change the world.

Dante's next attempt to push his vision came on Saturday, September 7, 1968, with the World Fighting Arts Championship Tournament, to be held at the Chicago Coliseum.

As part of her promotional activities, the attractive former Playboy Bunny was often used as a co-mouthpiece, a yin to Dante's yang.

In an article in the *Chicago Tribune* in August 1968, Anders told the reporter, David Condon, that she had used the confidence she'd developed through martial arts to fend off a man who'd been stalking her as she walked near South Shore High School.

As the man grew close, Anders turned on him. "You're going to get it. I'll kill you," she told the would-be attacker.

As she told the story, Condon wrote, "her hazel eyes, actually very glamorous eyes, became glowing coals."

Anders also said that she put up some of her own money to help get the event off the ground.

"I knew nothing about martial arts other than what I learned from him," Anders said. "I never had a black belt, but he had me on television. It was 'the Playboy Bunny with the black belt,' and it was big press. It was better press for him with me than it would've been without me, I guess."

The tournament was slated to showcase a full array of combat styles: boxing, wrestling, judo, karate. All matches would be full contact. Anders was quoted in the *Tribune* saying that they were planning to invite local resident and boxing champ Cassius Clay—soon to change his name to Muhammad Ali, to join the fray.

"We're going to march on his house," Anders was quoted as saying in the *Tribune* story. "Just for fun. We *really* think he might participate!"

Clay never showed.

And neither did the crowds the couple had expected. Compared with the packed house he'd produced in 1964 while working with Robert Trias, the crowd was an embarrassment.

After the 1968 tournament didn't reach the heights he'd envisioned, Dante's spirits plunged. He started taking out his frustrations on

Anders. The first time Dante gave her a black eye, she thought it would never happen again. But the abuse continued and became worse, Anders said.

Anders remembered her hand trembling as she used a straight razor to shape Dante's beard into the signature swoops and points, a job she'd perform every two or three days. If she missed or flubbed a part of the intricate design, she would fill it in with eyebrow pencil.

Meanwhile, Anders practiced her katas and karate forms, fearing with each movement that if she made a mistake, Dante would hit her. He encouraged her to use amphetamines in the daytime and sleeping pills at night like he did.

Anders doesn't recall exactly when she finally started pushing back. But he was a stubborn man. The more she pushed, the angrier he became.

One night, she raised the courage to tell him of her unhappiness. He suggested they go out and have a few drinks.

Back home after several Manhattans, Anders started crying and became inconsolable. There was a scene. She demanded to be taken home to her parents' place. Their reignited love had lasted some two and a half years.

After that night, the affair was over. Though Dante would randomly show up at her parents' house, "just to make sure I knew he was still around."

One night he came to the door and just stood there, speechless. He looked sad.

"I told him to leave," Anders recalled, "but he said, 'I want you to make me breakfast.' When I told him to leave, he threatened to hurt my father.

"So I made him something to eat and he left," Anders said. "After that, I pretty much just saw him in my nightmares."

THE DOJO WAR

One night in mid-April 1970, at Dante's request, Edgell covered a couple classes at Dante's dojo. Once he was finished, because he was in the general vicinity, Edgell paid a visit to Koncevic's dojo, arriving right around closing time. Being part of Dante's circle, and estimable fighters each, they knew one another well and enjoyed each other's company.

The pair retired to a tavern across the street.

"We had a couple beers and Koncevic was telling me how great John was, how long he'd studied under him, what all he learned from him, about both martial arts and living life. He thought so highly of John. It was kind of touching," Edgell remembered.

About a week later, on Thursday, April 23, 1970, Dante picked up the phone, called the Green Dragons' dojo, known as Black Cobra Hall, and issued the following warning: "I'm coming over there and I'm bringing a bunch of guys to bust up your joint."

To this day, nobody knows exactly what set Dante off.

Maybe it was about face—someone questioning Dante's ability to hold his own in a real fight. Or maybe it was about a woman, given Dante's rotating cast of companions. . . .

Or maybe it was because the growling dragon seal Dante used for his Black Dragon Fighting Society and his mail order business looked *very* similar to the Green Dragon Society logo, another dojo in Chicago, as interest in martial arts grew through the 1960s.

Or maybe it was because, as suggested by a source to *Black Belt* magazine, that the dojo war was touched off because Dante didn't like having perceived imitators—and sought to extort the Green Dragon Society for a turf tax. The Green Dragons trained hard. They would use blindfolds and weapons in their training, and they also used a technique where they would tap into an animal state while fighting.

Only Dante would know why he picked up the phone.

After that call to the Green Dragon Society, Dante called his students (and sometime instructors) Jim Koncevic and Michael Felkoff and invited them to go with him to Black Cobra Hall to confront the Green Dragons.

In turn, Koncevic, a decorated judo champion, called several students from his own school, the Tai-Jutsu School of Judo and Karate.

Though no one had any clue as Dante's motivation, their loyalty to the master was unwavering.

Koncevic brought three of his students with him to Dante's dojo. He initially told them they would be going out for a beer and a sandwich. Felkoff arrived shortly thereafter. Later, Felkoff would claim he had joined Dante's forces with the intention of mediating any beef that might arise.

At around 10 p.m., Dante and his crew arrived at the Black Cobra Hall, 3561 West Fullerton Avenue. Dante knocked on the large, castle-like door that was the entrance.

"Police!" Dante yelled. He carried with him a fake badge to bolster his ruse.

The door opened, and the six men went in.

Inside were at least six members of the Green Dragons, armed with the weapons that usually hung, as in the times of heraldry, on the walls of their hall. One man brandished a mace. Another held what was described in news reports as a sabre. Some accounts of what happened describe Dante and Felkoff going into a back office to talk to the school's manager. Others say Dante was in the manager's office unaccompanied when the melee touched off.

According to an article written by Massad Ayoob and published in *Black Belt* magazine in 1976, no one said for certain exactly how the fight started. But once underway, Koncevic grabbed a Green Dragon member, later identified as Jerome Greenwald, by his shirt and swept his legs, taking him to the ground with a judo throw called an *osoto gari*.

As the fighting escalated, Dante's crew tried making their way back toward the office. Koncevic was cut several times as he fended off attacks from blades, the melee encircling him. Jose Gonzalez, one of the Green Dragons, was cut above his left eye. According to a *Chicago Tribune* article, Gonzalez was later sent to a hospital where doctors tried unsuccessfully to save the eye. Later, Dante would claim he had himself taken out Gonzalez's eye.

According to Ayoob, after the fighting continued for a time, Koncevic ordered his group to retreat, screaming, "Let's get the fuck outta here!"

The students found the entrance locked and forced their way out, finally reaching the street. That's when they noticed that Koncevic was not with them. One went back inside and saw Koncevic flailing toward the door, his clothes drenched in blood. Ayoob wrote that the same man Koncevic had tossed at the beginning of the battle had thrown a spear at Koncevic, hitting him in the neck just before he got to the door.

Koncevic finally was able to stumble outside, where he collapsed onto the sidewalk.

One of Koncevic's students went to a fire station near the Black Cobra Hall and called the police. They arrived just in time to apprehend Dante and his fellow assailants as they were attempting to flee the scene. Ten men were taken into custody, including Count Dante.

According to *Black Belt*, Dante's loyal student and friend, Koncevic, was stabbed or cut thirty-six times, suggesting either a fight or an out-of-control assailant. He was declared dead at the hospital as a result of his wounds.

According to the *Tribune*, the ten men taken into police custody were questioned for two hours. Jerome Greenwald was reported as having told police Koncevic hit him in the back and knocked him down. He also alleged that Koncevic, in effect, killed himself. He said that that while down on the floor, Greenwald had grabbed a sword abandoned nearby a split second before Koncevic launched himself in attack; in classic movie style, Koncevic was summarily impaled on the blade.

Greenwald was charged with involuntary manslaughter. Dante was charged with assault and battery.

The incident soon became known as the "dojo war." To cognoscenti as well as to the uninitiated, it was a spectacular story, a bit of salacious news that fed the already-growing interest in martial arts. In an article in *Official Karate*, Dante was said to have claimed responsibility for "removing both eyes from the face" of one of his Green Dragon adversaries. Other accounts had that injury being caused by a pair of nunchucks wielded by one of Koncevic's students.

Accounts differ on Dante's true role in the fight. One witness's account suggested Dante was hiding under a desk.

On the night of the dojo war, while it is not clear whether Dante had called Edgell to join his crew, it is clear that Edgell would have been unavailable. Before and after he had met and studied martial arts under Dante, Edgell had served the Lord as a Baptist minister. On that fated Thursday night, Edgell was leading prayers at a church.

The next day, Chicago police came to Edgell's home to question him, but he was not there. They spoke to Edgell's wife; upon his return, she filled in her husband.

Stunned by what had happened—and that police would suspect a god-fearing man like himself—a preacher!—would have participated in such a brawl, Edgell went to a nearby police station to find out what was up and why he was wanted for questioning.

"They took me up to a room like you see in TV. It was kind of funny in a way. And they asked me if I had been present at Black Cobra Hall during the fight and I told them, 'No.'

"But the police didn't believe me," Edgell continued. "They told me, 'We happen to know you were there.'

"And I asked, 'How do you know I was there?' "

Edgell's interrogators claimed they asked around at several karate schools near Dante's dojos, and that his name was the first to come up. "If anyone was there, Woody was there," was the consensus, police said.

During the course of the interrogation, it became clear to Edgell that police believed Dante had killed Koncevic.

Being a man of the cloth, Edgell felt obligated to explain to the police why their theory made no sense. Dante would *never* harm his loyal friend and student. Fuck around with someone close? Certainly. He thought of himself as a big jokester. But never would he harm a loyal soldier.

Later, police would confirm Edgell's presence at church. Apparently, they also took to heart what he'd said about Dante and Koncevic.

"About a year after this all happened," Edgell remembered, "John called me up and thanked me. Apparently, one of the police had told him that one of the main reasons police dropped him as a possible suspect in Koncevic's murder was primarily because 'a priest stood up for him me and said there was no way I could have killed Jim.' "

When Edgell asked Dante what the catalyst for the incident had been, Dante explained that a Green Dragon member had been bad mouthing him all over town, telling people Dante was a phony and making slurs against his dojo.

Edgell recalled Dante telling him: "All I wanted to do is the same thing we did in the old days when someone was talking shit—go over to his dojo and visit him. You think I'm such a phony? Here's your chance to prove it. We could have put an end to that shit right then and there."

Despite the bravado, Edgell could hear the hurt still in Dante's voice.

"John told me, 'If I'd thought this would happen to Jim, I would never have gone over there that night.' "

According to documentarian Webb, Dante was distraught over the death of Jim Koncevic. "Through the years it became clear that the Count didn't much like to be alone. He needed a foil, a companion, a buddy to share adventures with."

In his *Black Belt* series on Dante, Massad Ayoob wrote that Koncevic's death "crushed Dante. Talking with (Dante) years later, you could tell that the death of his acolyte had broken a part of him that never quite healed."

MEETING BOB COOLEY

Though police came to believe that Dante was not responsible for Koncevic's death, Dante was charged with aggravated battery and assault for his role in the dojo war.

Hanging over his head were additional charges. According to accountability statutes in the state of Illinois, Dante could be said to be responsible for Koncevic's death because he had initiated the brawl and invited Koncevic to come to it, thereby placing him in the circumstances that led to his death. Even though Dante hadn't held the weapon himself, there was a chance he could be found culpable for the death.

Needing to lawyer up, Dante made an unusual, if not calculated, choice. He tapped Bob Cooley, a Chicago police officer who'd recently graduated from night law school. Later in his career, Cooley would work with law enforcement as an informant to bring down several top figures in the Chicago Outfit.

Cooley had police blue in his blood. His father and grandfather were decorated Chicago police officers, as were four of Cooley's brothers. But Cooley wanted more. In the late summer of 1970, Cooley had just completed law school and taken the bar exam but hadn't received the test results; he still had his day job as a police officer working in Chicago's Eighteenth District along Market Street.

Cooley was on the street working a shift when he got a call from the station telling him to come in because he had a visitor.

"The first meeting with John should have indicated how bizarre it was going to be," Cooley would later say.

When Cooley entered the precinct house, Dante was waiting, dressed "in a yellow fishnet leotard and a purple cape," Cooley remembered. Ignoring the looks of his colleagues, Cooley walked Dante to an office where they could speak privately.

Dante wasted no time: "I've heard that you're a tough son of a bitch, and you're bright and connected. I'd like to hire you to represent me."

Cooley tipped back his hat. He was looking at his first possible client. "I'm assuming I'll pass the bar, but if I don't, I know a number of lawyers who could help you."

Cooley later wrote—in his book, *When Corruption Was King*, about his experience as a cop, lawyer, and mob informant—that he truly believed he could help Dante with the dojo war charges.

Dante, assured of Cooley's lawyering skills even without bar exam results, produced $5,000 in cash and held it out to Cooley. "I want to retain you right now."

Taking the stack of bills in his hand, Cooley couldn't help but think his decision to change careers had been an auspicious one. As he would later remember: "Shit, I was only making $5,600 *a year* as a cop."

That night the pair met for dinner, and after that they were seemingly inseparable, two on a mission to party.

Dante brought Cooley to the Playboy Club for regular Friday night parties—a great source of networking for the new attorney; there were even a couple of Bunnies who needed legal work done and plenty of other people with deep pockets. Dante would also take Cooley to clubs and parties on the South Side where they'd be the lone white faces in the crowd.

Dante's trial convened about eight months later, in early 1971. Cooley opted for a bench trial, hoping a single judge could be more easily swayed in this case than a jury. Surely, he believed, a judge would understand that Dante was defending himself. In evidence were photographs of the assortment of weapons hung on the walls of the Green Dragon's dojo. Reports indicated one assailant had come at Dante brandishing a mace.

"As the prosecution put their case on, a lot of indications were given that it was just a crazy melee that ended badly," Cooley said.

The judge was "an old time Irish guy" who showed disdain for all the involved parties, not just Dante. Cooley said he could hear the judge muttering under his breath "they're all crazy" when they paused for breaks during the hearings. It was just the sort of reaction he was hoping for.

The Cook County Circuit Clerk's archives office said no records exist today of the dojo war court case. Peter Mikalajunas, a relative of Jim Koncevic, got the same empty result when he requested records from the court in 2008.

The judge dismissed all the charges.

"They're *all* guilty!" the judge exclaimed, exasperated. "All these people are a bunch of lunatics who deserve what they got." He brought the gavel down hard. "Now get out of my courtroom!'"

Dante grabbed Cooley in a bear hug and told him, "I've only had two people in the world that I love, my father and you. Not even my father could have done what you did."

"I CAN CATCH A BULLET IN MY BARE HAND."

Looking back on their long friendship, Cooley remembers how Dante introduced him to a world he'd never known as a longtime flatfoot from a modest family. There were nights at the Playboy Mansion and the Playboy Club. At all the South Side bars, everybody knew Count Dante; they were charmed by him, no matter how outlandish his boasts or his outfits, or how menacing he seemed. It seemed as if the more outrageous he acted the bigger rise he would get from people.

After all those years on the force, Cooley was on the ride along of his life. And then there were all the new clients who were coming his way, compliments of Dante's introductions. Dante liked introducing him as The Mechanic because he could fix any legal problem you had.

Equally dazzling was the endless procession of women.

"In the beginning it was great," Cooley remembered. "Then, after about two or three years, things started getting a little too bizarre. Dante loved to start fights. It's like, the way he dressed, he knew it would provoke people. They'd come after him and then he'd leave a pile of bodies behind. It was like his ritual. A fun way to blow off steam and break some heads."

One Friday night in summer 1972, Dante was driving down Dearborn Avenue in his brown Cadillac convertible, the one with his fanciful crest painted on the front doors. With him in the front passenger seat was Christa, the Stephens modeling school receptionist he started dating after his affair with Carrie Anders ended. Cooley was in the back seat with his date. The couples had been out to dinner, where many rounds of cocktails had been enjoyed.

Cooley had always had a soft spot for Christa; he didn't particularly like how domineering Dante could be with her. She once told him Dante treated her "like a slave."

"I would get mad at him because of the way he would treat her, not physically but emotionally," Cooley said. "He'd leave that poor girl to do all the work over at the adult bookstore in Old Town and put other side business responsibilities on her, but meanwhile, he'd be out partying and playing."

Dante had always been a player, with a steady supply of women culled from his salon and elsewhere. At one point, Cooley said, Dante shared an apartment with a pair of Playboy Bunnies. Dante's steady rotation of women continued even when he was living with Christa, Cooley said.

"She was so in love with the guy, she'd just do everything he told her to do."

As he drove on Dearborn, Dante kept turning around to talk to Cooley, meanwhile allowing the car to drift across the center line.

At one point, at a red light, he rear-ended the car in front of him. "Not real hard but he damaged it a little bit," Cooley recalled.

Four guys stepped out of the hit car, yelling at Dante, calling him all kinds of names.

"It's hard to describe the way he'd look when he was angry just before he'd get into a fight," Cooley said. "It's like a darkness washed over him. He'd get real quiet and focused. Almost like he was in a trance. Then his eyes would bulge and he'd explode."

At times, Cooley had seen Dante drop five, six, seven people at a time during bar fights, just using his hands.

"Everything would be so fast with him. One after the other, the way he would just put people down and they weren't getting back up. He'd leave people bleeding in a lot of ways. And after a couple of seconds, the fight is over. Nobody else wants to come anywhere close."

This time, however, when Dante stepped out of his car and assumed a fight stance—with hands like claws in front of his face and legs spread to form a solid base—the four guys jumped back into their car and took off through the red light, Cooley recalled. "I don't know if these guys knew him or the way he looked, he just scared the hell out of them."

Dante, Christa, Cooley, and his date arrived at Cooley's apartment at 70 West Burton in the Old Town neighborhood. They headed up to Cooley's apartment, but that darkness hadn't yet left Dante. Cooley wrote: "at one moment, Dante could be extremely sophisticated and artistic and the next moment crude and ridiculously macho." The potential for danger was always there.

The four were sitting and talking when Dante began prodding Cooley.

"Tell Christa how tough you are," Cooley recalled Dante saying.

"What?"

"Tell her how *tough* you are!"

"John," said Cooley. He'd use Dante's given name when he grew tired of the act. "Let's just relax, okay?"

Dante stood up and lunged at Cooley, swiped him across the face with his fingers.

"He barely touched me, but for a second I thought he might've broken my jaw," Cooley said.

Cooley gripped his face, his eyes trained on Dante for whatever might come next. What he saw was an immediate look of remorse that passed over Dante's face like a summer squall.

"You saved my life and look what I just did to you." Dante said, emotional. Clearly he was drunk, or high, or both.

He apologized to Cooley over and over . . . and then suddenly, he had a new idea.

"Where's your gun?" Dante asked. "You got it with you? Go get it. Load it. And point it at me."

Dante stood in front of the apartment's tall windows, squared his shoulders, raised his hands, ready to grab the bullet out of the air, a skill he had before claimed many times but never demonstrated.

"What? Are you *crazy*?" Cooley asked.

"No, I'm serious. I can catch a bullet in my bare hand."

"John, how am I going to explain this to the cops if I shoot you?" Cooley asked. Clearly his friend had gone over the edge.

THE CHICAGO OUTFIT

Throughout their friendship, Dante had harped on his pal Cooley to introduce him to players in Chicago organized crime. Known variously as the Chicago Mafia, the Chicago Mob, or the Outfit, Chicago's organized crime family dated back to the 1910s on the city's South Side.

Between his police and legal connections, the Chicago native Cooley knew plenty of players—for a time he would even work as a police informant. Thinking better of it, Cooley kept refusing to connect Dante.

"Dante and the Outfit? No way," Cooley said. It was like mixing fire and gasoline.

After the night when Dante had wanted Cooley to help him perform his dubious bullet-catching stunt, Cooley put some space between himself and the Count. They would still talk on occasion, but they were no longer inseparable, as they'd been for the previous two years or so, when they could be seen going out together two or three nights a week.

About six months after the incident with the bullet, in mid-1972, Cooley received a phone call about Dante. He was in trouble again.

After Jim Koncevic was killed, Dante found himself out of the martial arts business. His students left his schools, afraid to be connected to the volatile sensei. With his reputation tarnished, he didn't have the pull anymore to bring in the competitors and produce the tournaments that had been his triumph and his substance. Once a rising star in martial arts, Dante was now a pariah. He had gone to the dark side and few wanted any part of him anymore. Though he tried to make a go of it, he was eventually forced to close all of his schools in Chicago.

No matter. From an early age, Dante had always found ways to make money. No one could ever stand in his way.

He turned his attention toward the mail order business, selling his pamphlets and swag at a good clip. He also became a partner in a used car lot on Cicero Avenue on the South Side. In addition, he focused on his bookstores, one type offering adult (X-Rated) titles and products, another geared to the occult.

The adult store did particularly well. "In the '70s, people would make a fortune in these bookstores," Cooley said. "It was the only place you could buy X-rated films."

One of the big moneymakers for Dante was a large bookstore in Old Town, a northside Chicago neighborhood near Lake Michigan that was a counterculture center during the 1970s. Dante had muscled out the previous owner without paying a dime.

Like many of the businesses in that sector, the previous owner had for years regularly paid "street taxes" to the Outfit, Cooley said. Figuring he'd already paid for protection against the likes of Dante, the previous owner went to his Outfit contacts for relief. Let them do their job as advertised, the owner thought.

Confronting Dante about the bookstore fell on Jimmy "The Bomber" Catuara and his crew. Catuara got his nickname during the 1930s after he learned to use explosives under the tutelage of James "The King of Bombers" Belcastro. Belcastro earned his moniker in part by blowing up Chicago bars that wouldn't buy their booze from Al Capone. Catuara operated out of a grocery store that served as a front for the Outfit. In 1933, Catuara was caught with a seven-stick dynamite bomb and spent eight years in prison. When he got out, he went back to the Outfit and kept working his way up the leadership, serving as a bodyguard for Frank Ferrara among other duties. By the 1970s he was considered a high-level boss, running both loan sharking operations and the chop shops where stolen cars were converted into parts.

Catuara's crew included Sam Annerino, Catuara's right hand for the stolen car racket who also collected loan payments through force when needed. Pete Gushi also worked under Catuara, with a history that included hijacking, drug dealing, and fencing stolen goods. In 1961, Gushi was incarcerated at the US Penitentiary in Leavenworth, Kansas, awaiting trial for transporting $75,000 worth of stolen goods, when he tried to hang himself with a bedsheet. When the sheet tore prematurely, Gushi fell to the floor and survived. He later stood trial, was found guilty, and did the time.

Knowing they couldn't beat Dante with fists alone, Annerino and Gushi showed up at Dante's used car lot with shotguns.

That's when Cooley got the call to sort it out before someone was killed.

"They thought I was a policeman when I showed up," Cooley said. "They were demanding my ID."

As it turned out, Cooley had ties to someone much higher in the Outfit than Annerino and Gushi. For years he'd known Marco "The Mover" D'Amico, who would eventually work his way up to consigliere before he died in April 2020.

Cooley reached out to D'Amico to help sort out the business with Dante—to his surprise, D'Amico already knew all about the Count.

A meet was set a few days later at a motel bar near the Hawthorne Race Course, and the gunmen were called off, for the moment.

Cooley sat with Gushi at a table in a room right off a bar, leaving Dante briefly at the bar with Annerino.

"When I came back to the bar, here's Sammy with a fork in his hand. It's like they're comparing how bad-ass they were. As I'm approaching I hear Sammy say, 'I've pulled out eyes with these,' " Cooley recalled.

"Yeah?" Dante sneered. Curling his hands into his signature claws, as depicted on the cover of his pamphlet *World's Deadliest Fighting Secrets*, he said, "I pull them out with *these*."

In the end, Dante agreed to pay the original bookstore owner $25,000. Later, in private, Cooley chastised Dante for the brazen display of machismo. "Remember where that got you into the dojo war?" he reminded his former party pal and client. "Stay away from the Outfit," he admonished.

Unfortunately... and predictably... Dante did not take his lawyer's advice. The bookstore deal was only the beginning of Dante's dance with the Outfit. In the end, it may have been his downfall.

RAPKIN AND THE WHITE

In the early 1970s, right around the time Jim Koncevic was killed and Dante's life began to spiral, Arthur Rapkin's life changed dramatically as well.

As it happened, Rapkin was an early player in the soon-to-be burgeoning field of cocaine smuggling.

Long before routine baggage checks, X-rays, and drug-sniffing dogs, Rapkin found himself flying to Columbia, buying cocaine by the kilo, and smuggling it home in suitcases, most often through Miami International Airport.

The kid who once slept on mats in the back room of Dante's dojo (sharing the space with Aurelia, the lion) was now staying in five-star hotels, throwing money around in clubs on the Loop . . . and supplying stash to his sensei. And Dante was using it as quickly as he was getting it.

In 1972, Rapkin got married. Dante came to Milwaukee to serve as best man. The wedding was held in the bride's parents' backyard. During the official wedding photos, Rapkin and Dante made sure to be photographed together, striking various fighting poses. The display left some of the guests looking perplexed, watching the two men, dressed less for a wedding and more for a night out at the clubs, go through their poses. In one shot, Dante formed his fingers into claws, just like the magazine ads.

Soon after the wedding, Rapkin learned he was under investigation by both the FBI and the DEA, and that his phones were tapped. Regardless, Dante kept calling with entreaties to up his participation in the business. In Rapkin's mind, Dante was being completely uncool. Or perhaps he was just coke blind. Either way, it was clear to

Rapkin that Dante's continued brushes with law enforcement had no effect on his willingness to commit crimes.

"John wanted to be the guy in Chicago," Rapkin said. "He kept talking about getting in good with the Outfit. He was totally out of control. But what could I do? I owed him. Not only was he my sensei, he had taken me under his wing when I was just a kid with no prospects.

"It hurt me deeply, but at some point I had to just stop answering his calls."

FALL RIVER

After the dojo war and his other misadventures, Dante's name was shit in Chi-town. The martial arts schools were gone. The students were gone. Dante said he was broke. At one point he told *Black Belt* that he'd spent his considerable fortune on legal defense for his associates charged in the dojo war.

Accounts differ on when Dante first started corresponding with martial arts practitioners in Fall River, Massachusetts. He struck up a relationship with William Aguilar Jr. and others from Fall River who knew him by reputation.

John Creeden Jr., a Fall River resident who trained under Dante, said in an interview with Floyd Webb that he first saw Dante in advertisements in the back of Joe Weider bodybuilding booklets. (Weider is credited with putting bodybuilding on the map, starting the Mr. and Ms. Olympia contests, and so forth. In the style of the day, he, too, sold booklets and other swag via mail order.) Looking to go deeper into martial arts, but with few schools in Fall River to do so, Creeden said he and other martial arts colleagues sent Dante a letter inviting him to come to town. Dante responded and the relationship grew from letters going back and forth.

With his prospects in Chicago bleak, Dante eventually started training students in Fall River, including Aguilar and Creeden. Creeden said he and Aguilar were among the last ten people to be trained by Dante. The Black Dragon Fighting Society had a home in a dojo again.

According to Webb and Cooley, it was during one of Dante's trips to Fall River that he met Luigi DiFonzo, a man who also had expensive appetites and a brazen will.

DiFonzo, the son of a gas station attendant, had become a Boston attorney and investor. Like Dante, he was ambitious and aspired to more, though through riskier means than the Count. In the late 1960s, at age twenty-one, he made his first million from a bogus investment scheme, according to an *L.A. Times* article written by Robin Fields in 2000.

It would be the first of a lifetime of scams with which DiFonzo would be linked throughout his life. In the end, he would move his operations to Orange County, California, live a lavish lifestyle as a twice-jailed felon turned man of letters, FBI informant, and bon vivant with a fourteen-thousand-square-foot hilltop castle in ritzy Laguna Nigel. Known in Southern California as the Sicilian Gatsby, he would commit suicide in 2000, at age fifty-three, amid accusations that he swindled investors out of $40 million.

Close to when he met Dante, DiFonzo had fled Chicago for Fall River after being accused of swindling some two thousand investors in a commodities trading scam, according to the *L.A. Times*.

Like his new pal Dante, DiFonzo was looking for a fresh start.

Fire, meet gasoline.

THE PUROLATOR HEIST

In fall of 1974, Cooley hadn't seen Dante in more than a year. Dante would still call him up periodically and invite him to join him at the Playboy Mansion on occasion, but Cooley kept refusing.

One day, Dante showed up at Cooley's office, looking rattled. Gone were his cape and cane, his leotard. And his swagger—that was nowhere to be found, either. Instead, a Kool menthol cigarette was dangling from his mouth, getting smoke in one eye. He was bloated and sweaty. He couldn't sit still. He was a mess.

Cooley had watched Dante steadily decline. From the looks of him, Cooley imagined his appetite for coke was like his appetite for everything else.

"Bob, you know you're my dear friend," Dante said, a wild look in his eyes. "I'm going to give you a chance to win a million dollars."

"John—" Cooley began. He made a sour face. He was tired of the Count and his grandiose schemes.

"If I let you in on this, it's gotta be just between us," Dante continued, ignoring Cooley's face, his obvious annoyance.

"John, whatever you're doing, go do it, okay?" Cooley implored. "If I need money, I'll borrow some from you. But I just want nothing to do with it."

Right around the time Dante tried to rope Cooley into his plans, the Illinois Bureau of Investigation was tipped off that the Chicago Outfit was planning a big score.

The bureau started keeping tabs on Jimmy "The Bomber" Catuara, Pete Gushi, and Luigi DiFonzo, observing the three men as they met at a motel in Oak Lawn, Illinois, for about two hours on September 23, 1974, according to the *Chicago Tribune*. Catuara, who is related to DiFonzo, is credited with introducing him to Gushi. It was not noted in the report if Count Dante was among the group. While he was a known figure (and minor criminal) around Chicago and a big name in martial arts, Dante's only brush with federal authorities had been the blasting cap incident in 1965.

Almost a month later, around 1 a.m. on Monday, October 21, 1974, $3.8 million in small unmarked bills, and about $500 thousand in checks, were stolen from the warehouse of Purolator Security, Inc. at 127 West Huron Street. Purolator was one of the biggest armored car companies in America. It moved cash around the country, from businesses and banks to federal banking facilities. Because it could only move so many tons of money in a day, and because banks closed early, Purolator would regularly store clients' money in its warehoused vaults. Some nights, the huge safes were filled to the brim with cash.

To this day, the Purolator Heist of 1974 remains one of the largest such heists in US history.

As it happened, authorities were tipped off to the break-in when warehouse staff noticed a smoke detector going off in one of the vaults.

When firefighters reached the scene on West Huron, they found a fifteen-by-twenty-foot vault that had been scorched inside by a fire. The fire appeared to have been started by three plastic money bags filled with gasoline, each one lit with a long fuse. Authorities later said they believed the fire was meant as a distraction while the perps got away with the cash, which indeed turned out to be the case.

Eight other bags were filled with gas but weren't lit. A lack of oxygen in the vaults caused the fires to burn out quickly, but not before setting off the smoke alarm. Detectives said there were no signs of forced entry to the vault, which had concrete walls over a foot thick, a pretty obvious indication of an inside job.

According to news reports, the thieves were able to dismantle the burglar alarm, likely ignoring the smoke alarm on purpose. The timing for the heist was choice. In the vault was a week's worth of earnings from the Hawthorne Race Course. Also stored was money from downtown banks, due to be moved Monday morning. An additional $21 million in bank certificates were left behind by the thieves.

Initially, the perpetrators were able to stay ahead of the authorities. But a task force that teamed the FBI with local police soon picked up a trail leading to the missing cash.

The first arrested was Ralph Marrera, thirty-one, the only security guard on duty at the time of the break-in. He was arrested one week after the burglary at his mother-in-law's home in Oak Park. Suspiciously, he had refused to allow firefighters into the Purolator warehouse facility at first.

Within a day of Marrera's arrest, Gushi, forty-seven, was arrested as well. Interestingly, Gushi had visited Cooley's law offices only a few days before the heist. Later, Cooley learned that Gushi had hidden about $25,000 behind a sofa during his earlier visit, in anticipation of being arrested for the burglary. Gushi also left instructions for his attorney, with whom Cooley shared office space, to use that money to bail him out of jail should the necessity arise, Cooley said.

During the following two weeks, four more were arrested.

James "Jimmy the Greek" Maniatis was accused of renting the van that was used to haul the cash out of the warehouse. Police found chips of paint in the van matching what was used in the Purolator vaults.

Anthony Marzano, a thirty-three-year-old scam artist, and his cousin, Pasquale Charles Marzano, forty, a burglar alarms expert, also played roles in the heist. Pasquale Marzano was thought to be the mastermind, according to United Press International. Later they would both serve fifteen years in prison.

According to reports, the Marzanos had some time earlier persuaded their friend, Marrera, to hire on as a night watchman on weekends at the warehouse. With his help, the cousins were able to go to the warehouse prior to the robbery to search the offices of a senior officer of the company, where they found the combination to the vault's lock.

Apparently, according to the original plan, once the money was packed into bags and the fuses on the gas bags were lit, the van took off from the warehouse. The crew then moved some of the money into the trunk of a Lincoln Continental Mark IV that Luigi DiFonzo had rented from a company just outside of Chicago. DiFonzo, with Pasquale Marzano riding shotgun, drove the Lincoln from Chicago to a small airport in Port Columbus, Ohio. Gushi followed in his own Ford.

The three chartered a private plane, packed it with the stolen cash, and set off for the Cayman Islands, where they planned to stash a large part of the take in a "no questions asked" bank. But for some reason, the chartered plane landed short of their destination, in Miami. Altering plans on the fly, DiFonzo and Pasquale Marzano took off in another chartered plane headed to the island, while Gushi remained in Miami looking for a boat to take him to the Caymans.

DiFonzo and Marzano eventually got the cash to Grand Cayman, but the bank wouldn't accept it because it didn't have the staff necessary to count seven hundred pounds of small, unmarked bills.

After Gushi began talking to authorities, the case would eventually be wrapped up within a month.

Authorities found $1.4 million under freshly set concrete in front of Marrera's mother-in-law's house, where he'd been apprehended. Over the coming years of prosecution, Marrera would attempt suicide three times. Marrera would receive the stiffest sentence, twenty years. US District Judge John Grady said he gave Marrera the stiff sentence because he was "central and paramount" in the theft. "He was the indispensable person in this crime," Grady said.

Of the six people arrested, DiFonzo was the only one who walked outright, having been found not guilty of the two charges he faced, transporting stolen money and conspiracy.

Dante was questioned in connection with the case. He was given a lie detector test and passed. Some believe it possible his training in martial arts and meditation allowed him to game the lie detector, that he could will himself to believe what he wanted to and keep his vital signs calm enough to fool the detector. Dante was never charged in the heist. More than $1 million was never recovered.

The FBI says it has no records pertaining to any involvement Count Dante may have had in the Purolator heist.

As he remembers it, Cooley was driving when he heard on the radio that the Purolator facility had been hit. It was a block away from the last Chicago police precinct where he had worked as an officer.

"The moment I heard it, I thought, 'that must have been what the Count was talking about,' " during that fateful meeting when Dante seemed so strung out.

One night, sometime after the Purolator heist, Dante called Rapkin and spilled all the inside details of what happened at the heist. He painted himself as the mastermind. He told Rapkin who he introduced to whom, and who did what to pull off the crime.

"The names I don't remember, but the way it went down was like this," Rapkin said. "Somebody was a student of Dante's. That person knew somebody, and those people came to Dante because of his reputation. People wanted to work with him, even if they thought he was a little off in the head."

THE TAUNTON DEATH MATCHES

In the early 1970s, Dante reopened his Black Dragon Fighting Society, this time in Fall River, Massachusetts, where he'd found new acolytes who would accept him as their sensei.

In September 1973, Dante placed an ad in *Daily Variety* offering himself for acting roles. Bruce Lee had recently died. Perhaps he thought he could fill the shoes of the great actor and martial artist.

In March 1975, according to *Black Belt*, Dante was the guest host and "some said, silent partner in" the Taunton Death Matches, held in the Roseland Ballroom in Taunton, Massachusetts.

Writer Massad Ayoob went out to the Boston area on assignment to cover the matches and interview Dante.

Ayoob spent a couple of days in Fall River at Dante's Black Dragon Fighting Society. Ayoob couldn't help but notice that the dojo had, in one corner, a fully stocked bar with four stools.

Over the past fifty years, Ayoob has published thousands of articles in gun magazines, martial arts publications, and law enforcement journals. He is the author of some twenty books on firearms, self-defense, and related topics, including *In the Gravest Extreme* and *Deadly Force*, widely considered to be the authoritative text on the topic of the use of lethal force.

Never had he seen a bar in a dojo.

And never had he been greeted by his interview subject with a challenge:

"Do you want to go out on the floor?" Dante asked, meaning he wanted to fight.

Ayoob's first thought was to chart a path to the dojo's door in case this meeting with Dante went downhill and he had to fight his way out. Ayoob declined the fight invitation and told Dante he was only there to talk and get his side of things.

As the interview proceeded Dante was mercurial. One moment he'd be "aggressive and threatening," and the next he'd be his most charming, "all big warm smiles, your best friend."

One reason Ayoob had come was because Dante, who had all but disappeared from martial arts since the fatal night of the dojo war, was putting on his first event since Jim Koncevic's death.

Clearly Dante had turned dark. The name and intent of the event, The Taunton Death Matches, reflected Dante's state of mind. The rules allowed for anyone to come in, right off the street, and sign up for a no-holds-bared, bare-knuckle brawl.

"The rules allowed for, well, everything," Ayoob said, aware of the nihilistic vibe. "Thumbs in the eyes, groin kicks, testicle crushing . . . nothing was illegal. It was come one, come all, take your chances, professional and amateur alike, be prepared for anything."

Some believe that the Taunton Death Matches were among the first well-known attempts to create a mixed martial arts format like the UFC, which has become the most dominant fighting sport in the world.

To Dante, the Taunton Death Matches were just an extension of what he'd always taught: the reason to learn martial arts was to defend yourself day to day. As Dante had always loved to say: "You can't do a roundhouse kick in a phone booth."

"Dante said 'the place you're going to have to fight will not be a dojo,'" Ayoob said. " 'You're going to be in a bar. Or in the alley outside a bar. You're going to be three sheets to the wind. And the way I see it, if that's the way you're going to *play*, that's the way you should *practice*.' It actually kind of made sense. They even had two or three techniques that only worked on an opponent who was sitting on a bar stool."

Dante had a pair of students demonstrate. One took a seat on one of the bar stools set up in the corner at the bar. Another student grabbed the seated man by his shoulders and swept the stool's legs, knocking him and the stool to the ground.

"It's remarkably effective because the sitting man has no lower body flexion," Ayoob said.

In a second demonstration, the student seated on a stool employed a square-on punch to the testicles of the standing student.

Ayoob also saw Dante go through his paces. He remembers him as "skilled, very fluid, and balanced. No matter how vehemently people would speak against Dante and question his actual accomplishments as a competitor, no one could deny his skills as a martial artist. Not even his former sensei, Robert Trias," Ayoob said.

Toward the end of Ayoob's time in Fall River, Dante suddenly became agitated. He told Ayoob his lawyer would need to review Ayoob's article. He also demanded editorial power. He wanted the right to have Ayoob remove anything considered damaging to him.

"He was concerned about eventually being arrested in relation to Purolator," Ayoob said. "He was afraid that some Outfit people might kill him because of what he might know about it. He told me he locked himself in his condo at night with a shotgun across his lap."

Ayoob promised Dante he could look over anything that specifically mentioned him in connection with the Chicago Outfit and anything that might get him into trouble over the Purlator heist. But that was where his editorial feedback would end.

Hearing this, Dante pounded his fist on a table. "I'll fucking buy *Black Belt!*" he raged.

Ayoob just stood there and absorbed the tirade. After a few days in Fall River, he knew what to expect.

And just like that, a switch was flipped.

Dante calmed down, smiled big and put a hand on Ayoob's shoulder. "Don't worry. When I own *Black Belt* I'll make you the editor in chief," Dante said.

In retrospect, Ayoob said he got a sense from Dante that despite his new interests in Fall River, he knew his work in professional martial arts was coming to an end. He intimated that his life might soon end as well, and that William Aguilar Jr. was his designated successor.

Ayoob wrote at the end of his *Black Belt* series that his work "brings him into contact with many who have killed and such men give off a certain vibration. Dante had it, but whether he had acquired it in mortal combat or through expert mimicry, we may never know."

Ayoob also noted that Dante told him toward the end of his Fall River visit, " 'Ninety percent of what I told you is bullshit and 10 percent is true. Only I know which is true.' Then later he changed it and told me half was true, and half was bullshit. I think it was part of the persona, to keep people guessing. You can't have mystique without mystery."

PUROLATOR FALLOUT AND DANTE'S DEATH

In May 1975, about six months after the Purolator burglary, Cooley received a call from Dante. The Count wanted to see him.

Cooley hadn't spoken to or heard anything from Dante since he made his million-dollar offer. Frankly, he was avoiding him. His cocaine use and his grandiosity had become too much, even though he had a soft spot for the man who'd help jump-start his career.

Dante and Christa lived in a condo on Lake Shore Drive. Cooley brought a woman he was dating as an excuse to stay only briefly.

Cooley's date was starstruck. "This is really the real Count Dante?" she asked on the way to his place.

When Cooley arrived, Dante looked visibly different than last time they'd met. His trademark beard was not as perfectly sculpted. He appeared even more bloated; his color was off.

The four sat, drank wine, and talked. Dante appeared high.

"I want to show you something," Dante said to Cooley. Together the two men left the living room and entered the bedroom.

"You always thought I was a fuck-off. Look at this. *Look*!" Dante said.

In the closet was a large cardboard box full of hundred-dollar bills.

The two rejoined the women in the living room area, and soon Cooley and his date left the condo.

Cooley returned home at about 4 a.m. to find a phone message on his private telephone line.

It was Dante: "Bob, Bob, you've got to call me. What I showed you wasn't real money. It's all counterfeit."

The Deadliest Man Alive

Cooley called Dante back, assured him that he didn't care if the money was real or fake, and went to sleep.

The next day, Cooley got another call.

This time it was Christa.

"He's dead, Bob. I think someone poisoned him."

Cooley rushed over to the condo.

Dante was on the bed. There was no pulse. The body was cool. Cooley called a contact at a funeral home to take away Dante's body; they waited until he was picked up to call the police. A handful of prescription drugs were removed from the condo.

And the entire box of cash was missing from the closet.

To this day, about $1.5 million taken in the Purolator burglary has not been recovered. Cooley is sure Christa never had it; after Dante's death she was obviously without a source of support.

Cooley found Christa a job and continued to check in on her for the next few years. According to Cooley, he lost touch with her when she married again.

As for Cooley, he kept building his legal career. It was a sordid time in Chicago; Cooley was involved with some of the worst of the worst. Over time, he worked both sides of the fence, so to speak, representing both mobsters and politicians, some of whom were obviously in cahoots.

In 1986, Cooley was hired to represent Michael Colella, charged with attempted murder after beating Chicago police officer Cathy Touhy with an iron bar. Colella, who was believed to be associated with the Outfit, was acquitted. Cooley believed the judge in the case had been paid off by the mob.

Meanwhile, Officer Touhy went through multiple plastic surgeries after the beating.

Apparently disgusted by the case, the verdict, the blatant bribery, and the overall corruption in the city—most of it promulgated by the Outfit—Cooley went on to become a police informant.

Of course, the son and grandson of police officers wasn't lilywhite himself. Turned out he had a bit of a gambling problem and was deep in debt to an Outfit bookie.

In time, Cooley became the lead government witness in Operation GAMBAT, which eventually revealed what federal prosecutors described as a "movable feast" of public corruption, in which government officials are said to have conspired to fix everything from zoning cases to murder trials. As a result, a federal grand jury brought a wide range of criminal charges against five men, including a former Cook County Circuit Court judge, a state senator and a longtime Chicago city alderman. Four of those charged were convicted; the fifth defendant died awaiting trial.

According to news reports, Cooley gave government investigators upward of one hundred names of judges, police, and court staff who either accepted or delivered bribes to influence court cases. One of those bribes documented was the one given to the judge on Colella's trial.

After the GAMBAT indictments and subsequent trials, Cooley went dark.

In 2004, his book *When Corruption Was King* was published. Since then, he surfaces occasionally for interviews and is now working on a book rerelease and connected podcast.

But through his dangerous life, he's never forgotten about Count Dante, his charisma, his flaws, his everything.

"Somebody needs to tell his story," Cooley said. "I've never known anyone like the Count."

JUAN R. DANTE KEEHAN

"Sorry, I don't see any John Keehan in our system."

Keehan's death certificate had him named "Juan R. Dante" but with an "AKA Keehan" over his last name, and a burial location at St. Joseph Catholic Cemetery and Mausoleums in River Grove, Illinois. Staff at the cemetery didn't have a John Keehan listed in their files or Juan R. Dante, but did have "Juan R. Dante Keehan."

"Section S, Block 13, Lot 2, Grave 6. Nearby are headstones with the names Lococo, Thiel, and Emeringer."

Floyd Webb and I went out to see the site.

Cemetery staff left us a printed map with the grave marked and a QR code going straight to a pin in Google Maps.

We walked along the south corner of Section S, a plot reserved for small rectangular headstones that lay flat on the grave. Freight train horns sounded nearby over the traffic din of First Avenue. Otherwise, it was quiet, save for a few scattered visitors paying respects.

"It wasn't under trees, but I remember trees nearby," Floyd said as we walked.

He'd visited Keehan's grave before. When he saw that no stone had been left for Keehan, Floyd decided he would end his documentary by placing one himself. At the time, the surviving family members had to sign off on a stone to be laid but declined.

His grave was located as promised, three plots from the road that wrapped around Section S leading back to the mausoleum.

"Still no marker after forty-six years," Webb said. "Are you down there, John?"

"Are you *out* there, John?" I said.

"I still wouldn't be surprised if it came out he was living somewhere under a new identity," Webb said.

Webb had been working on his documentary, *The Search for Count Dante*, long enough to not discount seemingly impossible scenarios when it came to his film's subject.

Did Dante pull a D. B. Cooper, or Andy Dufrane, and live out the rest of his days lounging on a beach somewhere in the South Pacific? Not likely. He loved attention and was always pursuing both companionship and admiration. Living anonymously was never going to be his strong suit. Not for the rest of his living days.

When asked about the possibility that Keehan faked his own death, Bob Cooley is unwavering.

"I know a dead body when I see one," he said.

In 1975, Keehan's old friend Tommy Gregory attended Dante's wake at Barr Funeral Home and cried over his lost friend upon seeing him in an open casket.

But eight years later, in 1983, Gregory said, he received a strange envelope in the mail.

Inside the envelope, he found a Count Dante matchbook.

No note. No explanation. No postage or canceling. Just the pack of matches.

At one time the Dante matchbooks had been ubiquitous. In his zeal to self-promote, Dante had ordered thousands and left them all around town.

"At first I couldn't help but think, 'that son of a bitch is somewhere around here,' ", Gregory said. "It's exactly the kind of thing he'd do."

EPILOGUE

John Keehan/Count Dante lived his life as if he was in a street fight to the death. He was always calculating new ways to dominate—to win fights, to open new territories, to make money, to seduce women, to raise his profile. And above all, to live his life differently than the rest of run-of-the-mill humanity.

From his first time in a dojo, it was clear that Keehan had a talent for martial arts and a taste for domination. Skilled in boxing, karate, and other Asian disciplines, he quickly rose through the ranks of established martial arts schools and opened his own dojo by age twenty-four.

In time, however, the rising star would be ostracized by the martial arts establishment; his biggest offense, besides his personal flamboyance, was breaking the color and sex barrier, opening his dojo to Blacks and to women, some of whom would start their own martial arts schools, creating a lineage for people who otherwise wouldn't have had the chance to learn martial arts.

When not pursuing his interests in martial arts, Keehan dabbled in a curious assortment of other career pursuits. He worked as a hairdresser, skilled enough to be hired by Playboy Enterprises to coif the hair of its Chicago Bunnies. He worked as the director of a wig and hairpiece firm, and as a beauty consultant. Eventually, he would also own adult bookstores and other stores selling occult paraphernalia. His used car lot on Chicago's South Side was one of two enterprises that hinted at a connection between himself and the Chicago-based Mafia. The other, of course, was the Purolator burglary, which would come to be known the greatest heist in Chicago history.

As to the missing $1 million?
To this day, nobody knows.

To some, Keehan/Dante is remembered as a martial arts pioneer and a fighter against prejudice. With his free combination of styles and unleashed aggression, he helped sow the seeds for the type of modern mixed martial arts that is so prevalent today. A few years after his death, martial arts tournaments in all styles began upping the ante, allowing mixed martial arts and full contact. Today, as he envisioned, fighters from different styles face each other in Ultimate Fighting Championship's Octagon, the most popular fighting sport on the planet.

To others, Keehan/Dante was a selfish opportunist who took advantage of those around him, a peacocking, big-talking scam artist who always managed to stay one step ahead of the law. As he completed his transformation into Count Dante, his behavior became increasingly outlandish and dangerous. Throughout his life, the people closest to Dante would reach their limit with his antics and would distance themselves from him out of fear.

And yet, after he was gone, his legend continued to grow. Even if he'd stolen the Dim Mak, or made it up, he'd made it his own. That was Keehan/Dante in a nutshell.

Dante had been dead for about two years when Carl Eggerson, then ten years old and living on Chicago's South Side, saw his *World's Deadliest Fighting Secrets* ad in a comic book. Dante's looming afro and stylized face hair, his signature sneer, and his claw-like hands ready to deploy the Dim Mak left a lasting impression.

Eggerson, an introvert who found solace (and safety) in comic books, was exactly the type of person Dante had in mind when he placed his ad.

Today, Eggerson, a fifty-four-year-old Black man, holds black belts in judo, kung ju ch'uan fa, and chi ling pai gung fu, and is an instructor in kung ju, a mix of kung fu and judo.

Eggerson experienced one of Dante's visions for martial arts—integration in participants and in the styles taught, creating paths for anyone to develop new and more defense-applicable fighting styles. He didn't experience the prejudice in martial arts when he began training that Dante's students described in the 1960s. But Eggerson also saw how Dante's actions became a cautionary tale for martial arts schools in the 1980s and 90s.

The dojo war wasn't the only time a serious fight broke out between martial arts schools in Chicago and elsewhere. While other fights between schools didn't end in death like it did for Jim Koncevic, martial artists who came up in the 1970s and continued practicing into the 1980s did not want to see anyone else die as needlessly as Koncevic.

"The depiction of what you saw in 'The Karate Kid' movie, of schools against schools, they were still happening when I was coming up," Eggerson said. "They just weren't happening on an official basis because the schools by this time were all about business. They understood that if you want to stay in business, you can't go killing each other."

Likewise, there is Robert Bartkowski, who first encountered Dante in *Martial Arts: Traditions, History, People*, a 430-page exploration of the sport by Emil Farkas and John Corcoran.

Sitting on the floor of his local library, flipping through the pages of the massive book, "I come upon this picture, this guy with his claws out, and he's got the face with that jaggedy beard and this huge pimp metal on," Bartkowski said. "As an eight-year-old kid I was just entranced."

From there, Bartkowski began his lifelong martial arts journey in earnest. Today at age forty-three, he is a kung fu and tai chi instructor.

"I realized as I researched Dante further that what happened with me was exactly his goal," Bartkowski said. "How many people saw those ads and became entranced with even the faintest possibility that they could become so powerful as to kill with their fingertips? It's silly when you think about it, but he really could elicit that feeling, even with just an ad."

For all his foibles, Bartkowski said, the person Dante hurt the most was himself. A talented kid from a loving family with every advantage in the world, he became a sort of Icarus of the martial arts world.

"I think Dante is a classic example of someone who somewhere started believing his own myth," Bartkowski said. "Maybe the real message of his story is simply: don't believe your own bullshit."

WHERE THEY ARE NOW

Tommy Gregory continued to build his own contracting business after Keehan's death and left Chicago in the late 1970s to live near Phoenix, Arizona. He has since retired and still lives in Arizona.

Arthur Rapkin was serving a prison sentence in Mexico on drug trafficking charges when he learned about Keehan's death. Following his release, he left his crime life behind, became certified in acupuncture and other wellness practices, and chartered a new path as a healer and a health consultant. He is now retired and working on a book about his own life.

Bob Cooley kept working as an attorney for members of the Chicago Outfit and other nefarious clients after Keehan died. In 1986, he decided to become an informant for the US Organized Crime Strike Force to take down the Outfit. He wore a wire and provided witness testimony for Operation GAMBAT that served as the foundation for nine trials that all but decimated organized crime in Chicago at the time. Following the trials, Cooley wrote *When Corruption Was King* with writer Hillel Levin, chronicling his path from a Chicago police officer to mob lawyer and finally government informant. The book was published in 2004. Since then, Cooley has made a few brief public appearances, mostly to discuss the book and the subjects therein. Cooley is now working on a rerelease of the book with a companion podcast.

Floyd Webb is now working with Workaholic Production to release his documentary *The Search for Count Dante*, and he is gathering new footage for the film. Webb is also at work other projects, including working as researcher and script consultant on the Netflix

Africa project, Yasuke: An African Warrior in Japan, curating the streaming video channel bwcTV.tv, has recently founded the blacknussnetwork.com, and is organizing the 7th annual Afrofuturism film competition, AFRO5.

Carrie Anders' life took a more positive turn after leaving Dante. She became a realtor, bought a house with her parents, and tried to push him out of her mind. When news of Dante's death made local headlines, she got a call from a woman who had also dated Dante, whom she befriended. Not satisfied he was really dead, Anders called the funeral home to confirm. The wounds Dante inflicted remained with Anders even after his death. But she no longer had to wear the Playboy Bunny tail or assume the Dragon Lady persona. She could live life on her terms.

ACKNOWLEDGEMENTS

No story about John Keehan and/or Count Dante is worth telling without the knowledge, perspective, and wisdom of Floyd Webb. He was an unending source of support from shortly after I started this story until the very end. He remains the most knowledgeable person about Keehan I encountered throughout my work. I am deeply honored and grateful for his willingness to help distill truth in a story that's close to fifty years old. I saw firsthand how naturally giving and supportive he is to the world around him, even when he is at his busiest. And he's always busy. His endless energy and kindness are as inspiring as they are motivating.

Mike Sager, my mentor and editor, first helped me find my footing as a journalist and writer twenty years ago. He guided me through my early days at a newspaper and years after, showing me how to find grace and humanity amid people inflicting their worst inclinations on each other. Sager taught me how to "go the extra twenty-five more feet" when I was ready to tap out; he kept me on course throughout the array of challenges this story presented, pandemic-related and otherwise. He showed me many times that people can be tough and compassionate. His guidance and mentorship throughout this story were invaluable. I'm forever grateful our paths crossed and continue to be entwined.

Debbie Kaltman, my partner, was an endless source of support and motivation. I'm immensely grateful for her kindness and patience through the time it took to report and write this story. She too exemplifies how high standards can work together with compassion and provided the main foundation for me as I produced this story.

Thanks to my family who remain the best cheerleading section a person could hope to have in their corner.

Thanks to Massad Ayoob, whose detailed works on Dante for *Black Belt* laid essential groundwork and for being open to going over it all again with me. Thanks to Jim Kelly for his similar efforts and perspective.

Thanks to the people who spent hours upon hours talking with me about Keehan/Dante's place in their lives: Tommy Gregory, Bob Cooley, Arthur Rapkin, Woodrow Edgell, Michael Bertiaux, Robert Bartkowski, Preston Baker, Carl Eggerson, Alvin Linzy, Kenny Williams, and many others.

Major gratitude as well for Jean McDonald and her fine-tooth editing.

Finally, but far from least, thanks to John Schoenfelder for his patience and support.

ABOUT THE AUTHOR

Benji Feldheim is a Chicago-based writer and award-winning journalist whose work on crime, politics, music, food, and other life experiences has appeared in *Vice News, Crain's, Chicago Magazine, the Chicago Tribune, Mel Magazine,* and others. Feldheim, a University of Illinois graduate and onetime *Rolling Stone* intern, practices Brazilian Jiu Jitsu and plays drums in any bands that will allow him on the stage.

ABOUT THE PUBLISHERS

NeoText is a publisher of quality fiction and long-form journalism. Visit the NeoText website at NeoTextCorp.com

The Sager Group was founded in 1984 by award-winning journalist and best-selling author Mike Sager. In 2012 it was chartered as a multimedia content brand, with the intent of empowering those who create art—an umbrella beneath which makers can pursue, and profit from, their craft directly, without gatekeepers. TSG publishes books; ministers to artists and provides modest grants; and produces documentary, feature, and commercial films. By harnessing the means of production, The Sager Group helps artists help themselves. For more information, please see TheSagerGroup.net.

MORE BOOKS FROM THE SAGER GROUP & NEOTEXT

The Stacks Reader Series

The Cheerleaders: A True Story by E. Jean Carroll

An American Family: A True Story by Daniel Voll

Flesh and Blood: A True Story by Peter Richmond

An Accidental Martyr: A True Story by Chip Brown

Death of a Playmate: A True Story by Teresa Carpenter

The Detective: And Other True Stories by Walt Harrington

General Interest

The Stories We Tell: Classic True Tales by America's Greatest Women Journalists

New Stories We Tell: True Tales by America's New Generation of Great Women Journalists

Newswomen: Twenty-Five Years of Front-Page Journalism

The Devil & John Holmes: And Other True Stories of Drugs, Porn and Murder by Mike Sager

The Orphan's Daughter, A Novel by Jan Cherubin

Miss Havilland, A Novel by Gay Daly

Lifeboat No. 8: Surviving the Titanic by Elizabeth Kaye

Hunting Marlon Brando: A True Story by Mike Sager

The Swamp: Deceit and Corruption in the CIA (An Elizabeth Petrov Thriller) (Book 1) by Jeff Grant

A Boy and His Dog in Hell: And Other True Stories by Mike Sager

See our entire library at TheSagerGroup.net

www.ingramcontent.com/pod-product-compliance
Lightning Source LLC
Chambersburg PA
CBHW022008120526
44592CB00034B/743